MW00776675

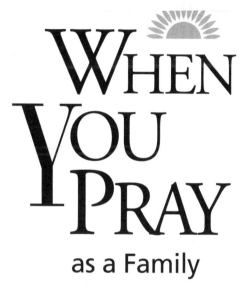

WHEN YOU PRAY

as a Family

Rueben P. Job and Leanne Ciampa Hadley

Abingdon Press
Nashville

WHEN YOU PRAY
AS A FAMILY

Copyright © 2010 by Abingdon Press

All rights reserved.
No part of this work may be reproduced or transmitted in any form or by any means, electronic or me-
chanical, including photocopying and recording, or by any information storage or retrieval system, except
as may be expressly permitted by the 1976 Copyright Act or in writing from the publisher. Requests for
permission can be addressed to Abingdon Press, P.O. Box 801, 201 Eighth Avenue South, Nashville, TN
37202-0801, or e-mailed to permissions@abingdonpress.com.

This book is printed on acid-free paper.

ISBN 978-1-426-70901-2

All Scripture quotations unless noted otherwise are taken from the *New Revised Standard Version of the Bible*, copyright
1989, Division of Christian Education of the National Council of the Churches of Christ in the United States of America.
Used by permission. All rights reserved.

Scripture quotations noted (NIV) are taken from the Holy Bible, NEW INTERNATIONAL VERSION®. Copyright © 1973,
1978, 1984 by International Bible Society. All rights reserved throughout the world. Used by permission of International
Bible Society.

10 11 12 13 14 15 16 17 18 19—10 9 8 7 6 5 4 3 2 1

MANUFACTURED IN THE UNITED STATES OF AMERICA

CONTENTS

Lent

Easter - Pentecost

Ordinary Time

Introduction

If your family is like most families, you and your kids live full and busy lives! Your days and evenings are filled with activities such as work, school, homework, sports, band, dance lessons, piano lessons, youth group, children's choir, scouts, meal preparation, volunteer opportunities—and the list could go on and on. I don't need to tell you that we are busy and active people.

Unfortunately, in the midst of our busyness, we sometimes find ourselves feeling disconnected as a family. We simply don't have many evenings when we are able to sit down to a family meal and share the events of the day. Quality time together seems to take second place to our schedules.

This weekly family devotional guide, based on the prayer guide *When You Pray: Daily Practices for Prayerful Living* by Rueben P. Job, is designed to help your family reconnect each week in a meaningful way by creating an intentional time together when you may read, explore, and discuss Scripture; pray together; and share the concerns and blessings of your week. It is our prayer that as you use this guide, your family will grow closer and be reminded of the deep love you hold for one another and for God. It also is our prayer that, by using this guide, you will be reminded of the deep love God holds for each of you.

This guide is designed for use by families with children of all ages. There are suggestions for use with both younger and older children and teens. Feel free, however, to adjust the format however you choose to meet your own family's needs. For example, if you have a child who is very young, you might not want to follow the entire format but simply choose the parts that best fit your child's needs. This guide is not meant to be a set of rigid rules but a tool to create a space where your family experiences God and reconnects in positive, loving ways.

To enrich your prayer experience further, teens and adults in the family may want to use the companion resource *When You Pray* as a personal guide for daily private prayer. You also may find it meaningful to include excerpts from the daily readings in your family prayer time together, sharing how a Scripture or essay or quotation has spoken to you. To learn more about *When You Pray* and other resources designed to help individuals and congregations grow in their practice of prayer, visit www.BecomingAPrayingCongregation.com.

The Main Goal of Your Family Time

Sometimes when we read Scripture or pray together, we want to make sure that our children "understand" everything and learn the "correct" lessons. Sometimes these concerns make us anxious, causing us either to stop praying and reading Scripture together or to correct our children when they share until they eventually shut down and stop participating.

Jesus said in Matthew 18:20, "Where two or three are gathered in my name, I am there among them." As we gather as a family, we invite and acknowledge that God is with us. The main goal of following this guide is to intentionally create times when God's presence is among us and between us. In that time, God is shaping, molding, and being present with your children. It is the creation of this sacred time, not the "right answers," that we strive to find.

By gathering together, inviting God to be in your midst, and by sharing and listening to one another, you create a holy space where God's presence is felt. Your children will become familiar with and accustomed to experiencing God's presence, and they will know how to find the peace and security that it brings when they need it later in life. Time and maturity will help your children find their adult theological stance and mature understanding of Scripture. While they are growing and learning, they are discovering what it is to be in prayer and to sit in the presence of God. This is the main lesson children need. The rest of the things they need to discover and know will be built upon this rock-solid foundation! As they share and you listen, they will become more and more comfortable being in the presence of God and will become confident that when they need and seek God, God will be there. If we fail to listen and spend our time being preoccupied with anxiety or correcting our children, they will doubt their own ability to seek and find God.

In this time together, I encourage you to trust that as you gather, God will be present. Simply enjoy being with your children, listening to and delighting in their insights and comments, and experiencing the sacredness and closeness of the moment. Try not to answer for them or correct their answers. It is better to have times of silence for quiet reflection than to always provide the answer. Let them ponder, and if they cannot answer a question, skip it. You never know: after they have had time to think about it, they may come to you hours later with an answer!

A Word About Intergenerational Sacred Time

Obviously, family prayer time involves people of different ages. Most likely it will involve adults and children or teens, but it also might include an infant or a grandparent who is living with your family. As you move through the activities, understand that some activities may seem silly for an adult or too difficult for a child. That is okay. Children learn through listening and watching. If they do not fully understand the question, allow them to share without correction; then have the adults share. The children still will experience the presence of God while learning that discussing our faith is an important part of our spiritual journey; and eventually they will grow into understanding.

On the other hand, parents and teens might feel that some of the activities are silly or that they are "too old" to participate in them. Never force a family member to do something he or she is uncomfortable with; instead, offer a gentle reminder of Christ's statement that unless we become like children, we will never enter the kingdom of God (Matthew 18:3). Just as children can learn from observing and listening to adults, so also teens and adults can learn from children. But to learn from them, we must participate in their world, which often includes doing things they like to do.

I encourage you to see this family time not as a serious time of focused reflection, but as a delightful time with your family and with God. There will be times of concern, times of joy, times of quiet reflection, and times of laughter. Relax and let God be in your midst.

An Explanation of the Weekly Readings

Each week your family will follow a similar pattern for your time together. Ritual allows us to become familiar with a pattern so that, rather than wonder what will come next or worry that we will be forced to share or do things that make us uncomfortable, we settle into the pattern and focus on "hearing" the Scripture and being present with God and one another. Ritual eliminates anxiety. Children love and appreciate rituals. That is why families have bedtime rituals and schools have class schedules they follow each day. Don't worry that your children will become bored with the ritual. The activities, discussion, and changing prayer requests will add variety while the ritual helps them to feel comfortable and even proud as they learn and anticipate the order along with you.

The weekly readings follow this pattern:

Week Number: The weeks are numbered from 1-52. We begin our journey during the first week of Advent and continue it throughout the seasons of the church year. (An overview of the seasons of the church year is provided on pages 15-16.) If you are starting your journey at another time, simply locate the appropriate season and begin there, or feel free to read the readings in any order you choose.

Theme: The theme for each week is selected from the Scripture passage and gives us something to focus on.

Supplies: Each week you will need a Bible, a candle, and matches or a lighter. You also may need one or more objects for the Family Share and Reflection Time (see on next page). All necessary supplies will be listed at the beginning of each weekly reading.

Welcoming God: Scripture often describes God as the "still, small voice." In our busy lives, it is important to make time for stillness and quiet. This step of the process is essential. I invite you to light a candle each week and sit quietly in its light until you and your family have slowed down and relaxed and are ready to focus on one another and God in the moments you will share together. (This segment is modeled from the section entitled "Becoming Aware of God's Presence" in *When You Pray*.)

Sharing With God: During this time, family members are invited to share anything that is making it difficult for them to slow down. Young children might share that they would like to be playing outside. You might share that you are worried about a project at work. Teens might share that they are worried about a grade. Simply share, making no comments and asking no questions. You can do that later. As you name your concerns, release them and let them go. (This segment is modeled from the section entitled "Inviting God's Intervention" in *When You Pray*.)

Listening for God: The Scripture lesson for the day is to be read aloud during this time. I suggest you invite family members to take turns reading the Scripture, reading from their own Bibles, if they have them, when it is their turn. Or you might have a different family member read the Scripture passage each week. This will help them to realize that God's Word belongs to all of us, whether we are young or old. You also might want to read from Bibles that have been passed down from family members who have died, such as the Bible that once belonged to your grandmother. This will remind your family that the Word of God is forever, from generation to generation. (This segment is modeled from the section entitled "Listening for God's Voice" in *When You Pray*.)

Family Share and Reflection Time: Each week your family will be given a suggestion for an active way to explore the Scripture together, followed by a few questions. Remember that the questions are there to help you express yourselves and to create space for listening. They are not intended to be a quiz. If a conversation develops that strays from the questions, great! Let it unfold naturally and enjoy being connected with those you love!

Asking God: This is a time of prayer based on the common prayer service found in *The United Methodist Book of Worship*. During this time your family will pray for the world, the church, your friends and community, your family, and your own specific needs. There will also be space for recording prayer requests each week, which you can choose to review the following week. (This segment is modeled from the section entitled "Making Our Requests Known" in *When You Pray*.)

Offering Ourselves to God: This is a unison prayer spoken by your family that offers yourselves to God and God's work in the world. The first few weeks you might need to say the prayer line by line and have family members repeat it, but soon everyone will know it and be able to recite it by heart. (This segment is modeled from the section entitled "Offering of Self to God" in *When You Pray*.)

Blessing One Another: Blessings are an ancient and biblical way parents often prayed for their children and one another. A blessing is simple. You take the hands of another person, look him or her in the eyes, and say whatever is on your heart. Your blessing might be something such as, "May God bless you, guide you, and be with you, today and always. In the name of Christ, Amen." Or it might be more personal, such as, "I know you are struggling in math class, and I pray God will give you wisdom and patience until you figure it out." Or it might be something simple like, "I love you, and I ask God to bless you!" Sometimes a blessing might have no words at all. You might simply hug a family member while saying a prayer in your heart or mind. There is no right or wrong way to bless another person. The important thing is that you communicate your love and care for the person, asking God to be with and to bless the individual. (This segment is modeled from the section entitled "Blessing" in *When You Pray*.)

A Final Word

We do many things together as families each week—we eat together, play together, watch television together, do chores together, go places together. Yet one of the most important things we can do together is spend time together in prayer.

It is our hope and prayer that God will give you the energy, discipline, and commitment to make this guide part of your weekly family routine. *Enjoy* the time you spend together reading Scripture, reflecting, and praying together. View it as a gift from God—for that is what it is!

May God bless you and your family as you spend time together in God's presence.

Overview of the Seasons of the Church Year

Advent

The first season in the liturgical year is Advent. Advent begins four Sundays before Christmas and ends on Christmas Eve. It is a time of preparation and expectation, focusing on awaiting the birth of Christ, as well as his second coming. This period of waiting is often marked by the Advent Wreath, a garland of evergreens with four candles. Each candle represents a theme of the Christmas season—usually hope, faith, love, and joy.

Christmas

Next is the Christmas season, which celebrates Christ's coming among us in human form. Christmas begins December 25 and lasts for twelve days, hence the traditional Twelve Days of Christmas.

Epiphany

Epiphany begins January 6. The term *epiphany* means "to show" or "to make known." It commemorates the coming of the wise men bringing gifts to the Christ child, thus "revealing" Jesus to the world as Lord and King. In some countries, Epiphany is the day that gifts are exchanged instead of Christmas Day, symbolizing the gifts given to the baby Jesus. The season of Epiphany is observed until Ash Wednesday.

Lent - Holy Week

The Season of Lent begins 40 days before Easter. The Sundays in Lent are not counted as part of the 40 days because Sundays are always a joyful celebration of the Resurrection. Like Advent, Lent is a time of preparation. During this time, we reflect and repent in preparation for the coming celebration of Easter.

The last week in Lent is Holy Week, when we commemorate the events of the final days of Jesus' earthly life. Palm Sunday commemorates Jesus' triumphal entry into Jerusalem, Maundy Thursday commemorates Jesus' institution of Holy Communion at the Last Supper, and Good Friday commemorates Jesus' crucifixion and burial.

Easter - Pentecost

Easter is the celebration of Jesus' resurrection. The date of Easter varies from year to year according to a lunar-calendar dating system. The season of Easter extends from Easter Sunday through Pentecost. Ascension Day, which celebrates Jesus' ascension into heaven following his resurrection, is 40 days after Easter Sunday. Pentecost is the fiftieth and final day of the Easter Season. It celebrates the sending of the Holy Spirit to the Apostles, which marks the birth of the church.

Ordinary Time or Kingdomtide
(Time After Pentecost)

The season after Pentecost, also known as Ordinary Time or Kingdomtide, begins after Pentecost Sunday and ends before Advent, lasting up to 29 weeks. In some faith traditions, the last few weeks of Kingdomtide have a distinctive focus on the coming of the kingdom of God, bringing the church calendar full circle.

LOOKING FORWARD

In days to come / the mountain of the LORD's house /
shall be established. . . . / Many peoples shall come and say, /
"Come, let us go up to the mountain of the LORD, /
to the house of the God of Jacob; / that he may teach us
his ways / and that we may walk in his paths."
—Isaiah 2:2-3

Supplies

- Bible(s)
- sacred candle, matches or lighter
- strand of yarn (about three feet long)
- blindfold

 ## Welcoming God

Gather as a family and light a candle as a symbolic way of inviting God to join you during this time together. Sit quietly for a moment so that everyone has the opportunity to relax his or her body, mind, and spirit.

Sharing With God

Say: If there is anything weighing on our minds and making it difficult to focus, let us share it now and then let it go.

Enter a quiet time when family members can share. You might go first and set the example by sharing anything that is weighing on your own mind.

Listening for God

Say: In the Scripture we are reading today, the prophet Isaiah describes how beautiful our world will be when everyone follows God and Jesus. This was written before Jesus was born, but we read it during Advent because Jesus showed us, through his life, how to follow God. Let us hear what Isaiah has to say.

Read aloud Isaiah 2:1-5. Take turns reading the Scripture, or have a different family member read the Scripture passage each week.

Family Share and Reflection Time

Say: Isaiah describes a beautiful world that we try to be part of as we follow Jesus. But it is not always easy to follow God and Jesus. Let's take a few moments and do an activity to remind us that it will take energy and focus to follow God.

Activity: Lay the strand of yarn on the floor in a wavy line. Invite each family member to walk it barefoot one at a time. Older children, teens, and adults should close their eyes or be blindfolded. Younger children, who are still learning to balance, will have difficulty walking it and should keep their eyes open. After each family member walks the yarn, rearrange the line to make a new pattern. Enjoy this time!

Discussion Questions:

- Was it easy or difficult to walk the line of yarn?
- What kinds of things does God ask us to do as we walk along the path God has marked out for us? (Examples: be kind to others, read the Bible, pray, forgive)
- What can keep us from doing what God wants us to do?
- Are there any changes we need to make so that we can walk God's path better?

 ## Asking God

Say: Let us pray together as a family . . .

Let us share our prayers for the world—for our country and leaders, and for other countries and their leaders . . .

Let us share our prayers for the church, ministers, and other spiritual leaders . . .

Let us share our prayers for our friends, teachers, and others in our community . . .

Let us share our prayers for family members and our own specific needs . . .

Use the space provided below to make note of family prayer requests. Each week, there will be a time to review requests from the previous week.

Prayer Requests:

_____

_____

_____

_____

_____

Offering Ourselves to God

Pray aloud together:

> God, we have read your Holy Word,
> We have prayed together,
> We have spent time with you,
> We have experienced your love for us,
> Now, we promise to love one another and others as you
>   love us.
> In the name of Christ. Amen.

Blessing One Another

Invite family members to bless one another. Some examples might be:

> "May God bless you, guide you, and be with you, today
>   and always. In the name of Christ, Amen."

> "I love you, and I ask God to bless you."

> "God loves you just the way you are, and so do I!"

(See p. 13 of the introduction for an explanation of how to give a blessing.)

Preparing the Way at Home

"Prepare the way of the Lord . . ." —*Luke 3:4*

Supplies
- Bible(s)
- sacred candle, matches or lighter

 ## Welcoming God

Gather as a family and light a candle as a symbolic way of inviting God to join you during this time together. Sit quietly for a moment so that everyone has the opportunity to relax his or her body, mind, and spirit.

Sharing With God

Say: If there is anything weighing on our minds and making it difficult to focus, let us share it now and then let it go.

Enter a quiet time when family members can share. You might go first and set the example by sharing anything that is weighing on your own mind.

 ## Listening for God

Say: In this second week of Advent, we are going to hear about John the Baptist, who was Jesus' cousin. John preached about Jesus being our Savior. He said that the people needed to prepare for his coming into the world.

Read aloud Luke 3:1-6. Take turns reading the Scripture, or have a different family member read the Scripture passage each week.

Family Share and Reflection Time

Say: John spoke in this Scripture about preparing for Christ. Advent is the four weeks before Christmas. It is the time when we prepare ourselves to celebrate that Jesus was born and that we can follow him.

Activity: Take a walk around your home and point out anything that reminds you that you are preparing for Christmas. Notice things such as your Christmas tree, if it is up, wrapping paper or presents, cards, decorations, and so forth. If you do not have any young children, you might choose simply to stay put and talk about evidences you have seen in your home and your community.

Discussion Questions:
- What things have we done as a family to prepare for Christmas?
- What things have you done personally to prepare for Christmas?
- Are there things we can do to make our spirits ready to celebrate?

Asking God

Say: Let us pray together as a family . . .

Let us share our prayers for the world—for our country and leaders, and for other countries and their leaders . . .

Let us share our prayers for the church, ministers, and other spiritual leaders . . .

Let us share our prayers for our friends, teachers, and others in our community . . .

Let us share our prayers for family members and our own specific needs . . .

Use the space provided below to make note of family prayer requests. Take a few minutes to review requests from the previous week.

Prayer Requests:

_____

_____

_____

_____

_____

Offering Ourselves to God

Pray aloud together:

God, we have read your Holy Word,
We have prayed together,
We have spent time with you,
We have experienced your love for us,
Now, we promise to love one another and others as you love us.
In the name of Christ. Amen.

Blessing One Another

Invite family members to bless one another. Some examples might be:

> "May God bless you, guide you, and be with you, today and always. In the name of Christ, Amen."

> "I love you, and I ask God to bless you."

> "God loves you just the way you are, and so do I!"

Do Not Be Afraid

The angel said to her, "Do not be afraid . . ." —Luke 1:30

Supplies

- Bible(s)
- sacred candle, matches or lighter
- crayons or colored pencils (or pens and pencils) and paper for each family member

 ## Welcoming God

Gather as a family and light a candle as a symbolic way of inviting God to join you during this time together. Sit quietly for a moment so that everyone has the opportunity to relax his or her body, mind, and spirit.

Sharing With God

Say: If there is anything weighing on our minds and making it difficult to focus, let us share it now and then let it go.

Enter a quiet time when family members can share. You might go first and set the example by sharing anything that is weighing on your own mind.

Listening for God

Say: This is the third week of Advent, and our Scripture is the story of the angel Gabriel telling Mary she is about to become the mother of Jesus.

Read aloud Luke 1:26-38. Take turns reading the Scripture, or have a different family member read the Scripture passage each week.

 # Family Share and Reflection Time

Say: When Gabriel appeared to Mary, she felt frightened. He told her, "Do not be afraid." We all have things we are afraid of. Let's spend a few moments in quiet and draw pictures or write about the things we are fearful of. They might be big things or small things.

Activity: Each family member is to draw a picture of something he or she is afraid of. Share the pictures with one another as you are willing. Then, one at a time, take turns drawing an "X" over your picture while family members say in unison, "Do not be afraid, (name of person), for you are loved by God!"

Older children and teens may prefer to write about what they are afraid of instead of drawing a picture. Then have them tear up or burn their papers instead of marking them with an "X." You also might encourage them to do this activity on behalf of others they know who are facing fears as well. Sometimes it is easier for teens to speak out for others than to share their own fears.

Discussion Questions:

- Mary was beloved by God. Do you have a hard or easy time believing you are beloved by God?
- Have you ever felt the presence of angels with you? If so, tell about the experience.
- Have you ever prayed when you were afraid? If so, how did it help you?

 Asking God

Say: Let us pray together as a family . . .

> Let us share our prayers for the world—for our country and leaders, and for other countries and their leaders . . .
>
> Let us share our prayers for the church, ministers, and other spiritual leaders . . .
>
> Let us share our prayers for our friends, teachers, and others in our community . . .
>
> Let us share our prayers for family members and our own specific needs . . .

Use the space provided below to make note of family prayer requests. Take a few minutes to review requests from the previous week.

Prayer Requests:

_____

_____

_____

_____

_____

Offering Ourselves to God

Pray aloud together:

> God, we have read your Holy Word,
> We have prayed together,
> We have spent time with you,
> We have experienced your love for us,
> Now, we promise to love one another and others as you
> love us.
> In the name of Christ. Amen.

Blessing One Another

Invite family members to bless one another. Some examples might be:

> "May God bless you, guide you, and be with you, today and always. In the name of Christ, Amen."

> "I love you, and I ask God to bless you."

> "God loves you just the way you are, and so do I!"

Spiritual Friends

*Mary stayed with Elizabeth for about three months
and then returned home. —Luke 1:56 (NIV)*

Supplies

- Bible(s)
- sacred candle, matches or lighter
- a number of other candles (tea lights, votives, or whatever other candles you have on hand)

 ## Welcoming God

Gather as a family and light a candle as a symbolic way of inviting God to join you during this time together. Sit quietly for a moment so that everyone has the opportunity to relax his or her body, mind, and spirit.

Sharing With God

Say: If there is anything weighing on our minds and making it difficult to focus, let us share it now and then let it go.

Enter a quiet time when family members can share. You might go first and set the example by sharing anything that is weighing on your own mind.

Listening for God

Say: This is the forth week of Advent. Our Scripture is about Mary going to see her cousin and friend, Elizabeth, after she found out that she was pregnant. She was scared and alone, and she turned to her friend for help and support.

Read aloud Luke 1:39-56. Take turns reading the Scripture, or have a different family member read the Scripture passage each week.

Family Share and Reflection Time

Say: Christmas is a time when we get phone calls, Christmas cards, and emails from people we haven't heard from in a long time. It also is a time when friends and family visit. The holidays remind us of how many loved ones we have. Now we are going to give thanks to God for our family and friends.

Activity: Invite family members to name people who are important to them. As a family member names a person, light a candle in his or her honor. Sit quietly in the light of friendship and love!

Discussion Questions:
- Was there anyone you didn't think of at first who came to mind as we were lighting candles?
- Which of the friends or family members you named would you go to if you needed help and support? Who would your "Elizabeth" be?
- What can you do during the holidays to let these people know how much you care for them?

Asking God

Say: Let us pray together as a family . . .

Let us share our prayers for the world—for our country and leaders, and for other countries and their leaders . . .

Let us share our prayers for the church, ministers, and other spiritual leaders . . .

Let us share our prayers for our friends, teachers, and others in our community . . .

Let us share our prayers for family members and our own specific needs . . .

Use the space provided below to make note of family prayer requests. Take a few minutes to review requests from the previous week.

Prayer Requests:

_____

_____

_____

_____

_____

Offering Ourselves to God

Pray aloud together:

God, we have read your Holy Word,
We have prayed together,
We have spent time with you,
We have experienced your love for us,

Now, we promise to love one another and others as you love us.

In the name of Christ. Amen.

Blessing One Another

Invite family members to bless one another. Some examples might be:

> "May God bless you, guide you, and be with you, today and always. In the name of Christ, Amen."

> "I love you, and I ask God to bless you."

> "God loves you just the way you are, and so do I!"

JOSEPH'S DREAM

*Now after they had left, an angel of the Lord appeared
to Joseph in a dream . . . —Matthew 2:13*

Supplies

- Bible(s)
- sacred candle, matches or lighter
- crayons or colored pencils
- paper

 ## Welcoming God

Gather as a family and light a candle as a symbolic way of inviting God to join you during this time together. Sit quietly for a moment so that everyone has the opportunity to relax his or her body, mind, and spirit.

Sharing With God

Say: If there is anything weighing on our minds and making it difficult to focus, let us share it now and then let it go.

Enter a quiet time when family members can share. You might go first and set the example by sharing anything that is weighing on your own mind.

Listening for God

Say: After Jesus was born, King Herod thought that Jesus was going to grow up and take over his kingdom. He became very jealous and ordered that all the male children who were age two or younger should be killed. But an angel of God appeared to Joseph in a dream and warned him to take Jesus and Mary and go to Egypt until it was safe for them to return.

Read aloud Matthew 2:13-15. Take turns reading the Scripture, or have a different family member read the Scripture passage each week.

 ## Family Share and Reflection Time

Say: In this Scripture, God appeared to Joseph in a dream. There are many times in the Bible where God speaks to people through dreams and visions.

Activity: Have each family member draw a picture of a dream he or she has had. It can be a dream they had while sleeping or a dream they have for the future—something they want to do in life, such as, "I dream of becoming a teacher someday." If teens are reluctant to draw pictures, encourage them to simply talk about their dreams. Share your dreams and enjoy!

Discussion Questions:
- Have you ever had a dream that you believe was a message from God, or a dream in which God was present?

- Do you have a dream that might become reality if the entire family helped you? What is it? How can we help to make it come true?
- Do you think we should pay attention to all of our dreams as messages from God? Do you think some dreams are from God and others are not? Why or why not?

 ## Asking God

Say: Let us pray together as a family . . .

Let us share our prayers for the world—for our country and leaders, and for other countries and their leaders . . .

Let us share our prayers for the church, ministers, and other spiritual leaders . . .

Let us share our prayers for our friends, teachers, and others in our community . . .

Let us share our prayers for family members and our own specific needs . . .

Use the space provided below to make note of family prayer requests. Take a few minutes to review requests from the previous week.

Prayer Requests:

_____

_____

_____

_____

_____

Offering Ourselves to God

Pray aloud together:

> God, we have read your Holy Word,
> We have prayed together,
> We have spent time with you,
> We have experienced your love for us,
> Now, we promise to love one another and others as you
>   love us.
> In the name of Christ. Amen.

Blessing One Another

Invite family members to bless one another. Some examples
might be:

> "May God bless you, guide you, and be with you, today
>   and always. In the name of Christ, Amen."

> "I love you, and I ask God to bless you."

> "God loves you just the way you are, and so do I!"

THE WISE MEN VISIT JESUS

*On entering the house, they saw the child with Mary
his mother; and they knelt down and paid him homage.
Then, opening their treasure chests, they offered him gifts
of gold, frankincense, and myrrh. —Matthew 2:11*

Supplies
- Bible(s)
- sacred candle, matches or lighter
- ball of yarn or twine

 ## Welcoming God

Gather as a family and light a candle as a symbolic way of inviting God to join you during this time together. Sit quietly for a moment so that everyone has the opportunity to relax his or her body, mind, and spirit.

Sharing With God

Say: If there is anything weighing on our minds and making it difficult to focus, let us share it now and then let it go.

Enter a quiet time when family members can share. You might go first and set the example by sharing anything that is weighing on your own mind.

Listening for God

Say: Epiphany is a holiday celebrated twelve days after Christmas; it is a time when we remember the story of the wise men visiting Jesus.

Read aloud Matthew 2:1-12. Take turns reading the Scripture, or have a different family member read the Scripture passage each week.

 Family Share and Reflection Time

Say: The wise men recognized how precious and wonderful Jesus is. This activity will help us remember how precious and wonderful we are to one another.

Activity: Stand in a circle. One person holds the ball of yarn, tells another member of the family how special he or she is, and then, holding on to a piece of string, throws the ball of yarn to that person. That family member compliments another family member and throws the yarn while holding onto the string. Continue in this manner, and before long you will have formed a web of love!

Discussion Questions:
- Why don't we share words of affirmation and love with one another more often than we do?
- How did it feel to be told how wonderful you are?
- Who in our family do you wish would tell you how wonderful you are more often?

 **Asking God**

Say: Let us pray together as a family . . .

Let us share our prayers for the world—for our country and leaders, and for other countries and their leaders . . .

Let us share our prayers for the church, ministers, and other spiritual leaders . . .

Let us share our prayers for our friends, teachers, and others in our community . . .

Let us share our prayers for family members and our own specific needs . . .

Use the space provided below to make note of family prayer requests. Take a few minutes to review requests from the previous week.

Prayer Requests:

_____
_____
_____
_____
_____

Offering Ourselves to God

Pray aloud together:

God, we have read your Holy Word,
We have prayed together,
We have spent time with you,
We have experienced your love for us,

Now, we promise to love one another and others as you love us.

In the name of Christ. Amen.

Blessing One Another

Invite family members to bless one another. Some examples might be:

"May God bless you, guide you, and be with you, today and always. In the name of Christ, Amen."

"I love you, and I ask God to bless you."

"God loves you just the way you are, and so do I!"

THE BAPTISM OF JESUS

Now when all the people were baptized,
and when Jesus also had been baptized and was praying,
the heaven was opened, and the Holy Spirit descended upon him
in bodily form like a dove. And a voice came from heaven,
"You are my Son, the Beloved; with you I am well pleased."
—Luke 3:21-22

Supplies

- Bible(s)
- sacred candle, matches or lighter
- small bowl of water

 ## Welcoming God

Gather as a family and light a candle as a symbolic way of inviting God to join you during this time together. Sit quietly for a moment so that everyone has the opportunity to relax his or her body, mind, and spirit.

Sharing With God

Say: If there is anything weighing on our minds and making it difficult to focus, let us share it now and then let it go.

Enter a quiet time when family members can share. You might go first and set the example by sharing anything that is weighing on your own mind.

Listening for God

Say: Today we will read about the day Jesus was baptized. Jesus was baptized in the Jordan River by his cousin John. We know him as John the Baptist.

Read aloud Luke 3:15-16 and 21-22. Take turns reading the Scripture, or have a different family member read the Scripture passage each week.

 ## Family Share and Reflection Time

Say: People are baptized in many different ways. Some are dipped completely under the water, some have water poured on their heads, some have water sprinkled on their heads, and some have the sign of the cross made on their foreheads. The important thing is not how we are baptized but simply that we are baptized. Being baptized is a time when we publicly declare that God is our God and we are welcomed into God's family of faith.

Activity: Have family members who remember their baptism tell about when and how they were baptized. If children in the family were baptized as infants, parents can share about the day they were baptized. If no one has been baptized, or if some family members have not yet been baptized, you might want to discuss whether anyone wants to be baptized. Then take a bowl of water, dip your finger in it, and make a cross on the forehead of each family member who has been baptized, saying, "Remember your baptism and give thanks!" For family members who have not been baptized, do the same, saying, "Anticipate the joy of your baptism and give thanks!"

Discussion Questions:

- Is your baptism something meaningful to you? Why or why not?
- What are some ways we might celebrate our baptisms as a family? (Examples: light a candle or have cake on the anniversary date of each family member's baptism)

 Asking God

Say: Let us pray together as a family . . .

Let us share our prayers for the world—for our country and leaders, and for other countries and their leaders . . .

Let us share our prayers for the church, ministers, and other spiritual leaders . . .

Let us share our prayers for our friends, teachers, and others in our community . . .

Let us share our prayers for family members and our own specific needs . . .

Use the space provided below to make note of family prayer requests. Take a few minutes to review requests from the previous week.

Prayer Requests:

_____

_____

_____

_____

_____

Offering Ourselves to God

Pray aloud together:

> God, we have read your Holy Word,
> We have prayed together,
> We have spent time with you,
> We have experienced your love for us,
> Now, we promise to love one another and others as you
>   love us.
> In the name of Christ. Amen.

Blessing One Another

Invite family members to bless one another. Some examples might be:

> "May God bless you, guide you, and be with you, today
>   and always. In the name of Christ, Amen."

> "I love you, and I ask God to bless you."

> "God loves you just the way you are, and so do I!"

COME AND SEE

Nathanael said to him, "Can anything good come out of Nazareth?"
Philip said to him, "Come and see." —John 1:46

Supplies
- Bible(s)
- sacred candle, matches or lighter
- slips of paper for charades with the following phrases written on them: "healed the blind," "loved the poor," "healed the sick," "was kind to children," "blessed people," and "told stories"

 ## Welcoming God

Gather as a family and light a candle as a symbolic way of inviting God to join you during this time together. Sit quietly for a moment so that everyone has the opportunity to relax his or her body, mind, and spirit.

Sharing With God

Say: If there is anything weighing on our minds and making it difficult to focus, let us share it now and then let it go.

Enter a quiet time when family members can share. You might go first and set the example by sharing anything that is weighing on your own mind.

Listening for God

Say: As Jesus began his ministry, he gathered some disciples to be with him and learn from him. Philip was very excited about Jesus and told Nathanael about him, who was skeptical and doubted that Jesus was anything special. So Philip invited Nathanael to "come and see" for himself!

Read aloud John 1:43-51. Take turns reading the Scripture, or have a different family member read the Scripture passage each week.

 Family Share and Reflection Time

Say: Jesus did many wonderful things. People saw the things that Jesus did and believed.

Activity: Play charades to name some of the things that Jesus did. Begin by using the slips of paper listed in the supplies list. Then, as family members remember other stories, let them act them out. All ages can have fun playing charades. Enjoy the time together!

Discussion Questions:
- Why do you think people needed to see Jesus do things before they believed?
- There is a saying, "Actions speak louder than words." What do you think that means? Do you agree?
- Do your actions speak louder than your words?

 **Asking God**

Say: Let us pray together as a family . . .

Let us share our prayers for the world—for our country and for our leaders, and for other countries and their leaders . . .
Let us share our prayers for the church, ministers, and other spiritual leaders . . .
Let us share our prayers for our friends, teachers, and others in our community . . .
Let us share our prayers for family members and our own specific needs . . .

Use the space provided below to make note of family prayer requests. Take a few minutes to review requests from the previous week.

Prayer Requests:

_____

_____

_____

_____

_____

Offering Ourselves to God

Pray aloud together:

God, we have read your Holy Word,
We have prayed together,
We have spent time with you,
We have experienced your love for us,

Now, we promise to love one another and others as you
   love us.
In the name of Christ. Amen.

Blessing One Another

Invite family members to bless one another. Some examples
might be:

"May God bless you, guide you, and be with you, today
   and always. In the name of Christ, Amen."

"I love you, and I ask God to bless you."

"God loves you just the way you are, and so do I!"

FOLLOWING JESUS

As Jesus passed along the Sea of Galilee,
he saw Simon and his brother Andrew
casting a net into the sea—for they were fishermen.
And Jesus said to them, "Follow me
and I will make you fish for people." —Mark 1:16-17

Supplies

- Bible(s)
- sacred candle, matches or lighter
- *optional for older children, teens:* blindfolds, dishcloths

 ## Welcoming God

Gather as a family and light a candle as a symbolic way of inviting God to join you during this time together. Sit quietly for a moment so that everyone has the opportunity to relax his or her body, mind, and spirit.

Sharing With God

Say: If there is anything weighing on our minds and making it difficult to focus, let us share it now and then let it go.

Enter a quiet time when family members can share. You might go first and set the example by sharing anything that is weighing on your own mind.

Listening for God

Say: Jesus recruited twelve men to be his followers so that they might learn from him and carry on his ministry after his death. Many of them were fishermen, and this is their story.

Read aloud Mark 1:14-20. Take turns reading the Scripture, or have a different family member read the Scripture passage each week.

 ## Family Share and Reflection Time

Say: These men and many women followed Jesus throughout his whole ministry. Now we are disciples, and we are called to follow Jesus. This game will help us remember that following Jesus is not always easy!

Activity: Play the game Follow the Leader, taking turns as leader. Then have everyone shut his or her eyes and try to play the game. They won't be able to follow.

For older children and teens, make the game a bit more fun by having them wear a blindfold. Then have the leader and the child or teen hold opposite ends of the same dishcloth. Take them places that are funny or challenging, such as under a table or over a couch. Have fun with it!

Discussion Questions:
- When we follow Jesus, we have to "keep our eyes open." What things can we do to stay focused on Jesus?

- When we closed our eyes, we could not follow the leader. What things keep you from focusing on Jesus?
- What changes could you make to help you stay focused on Jesus?

 ## Asking God

Say: Let us pray together as a family . . .

Let us share our prayers for the world—for our country and leaders, and for other countries and their leaders . . .

Let us share our prayers for the church, ministers, and other spiritual leaders . . .

Let us share our prayers for our friends, teachers, and others in our community . . .

Let us share our prayers for family members and our own specific needs . . .

Use the space provided below to make note of family prayer requests. Take a few minutes to review requests from the previous week.

Prayer Requests:

_____

_____

_____

_____

_____

Offering Ourselves to God

Pray aloud together:

> God, we have read your Holy Word,
> We have prayed together,
> We have spent time with you,
> We have experienced your love for us,
> Now, we promise to love one another and others as you
> love us.
> In the name of Christ. Amen.

Blessing One Another

Invite family members to bless one another. Some examples
might be:

> "May God bless you, guide you, and be with you, today
> and always. In the name of Christ, Amen."

> "I love you, and I ask God to bless you."

> "God loves you just the way you are, and so do I!"

THE BEATITUDES

When Jesus saw the crowds, he went up the mountain; and after he sat down, his disciples came to him. Then he began to speak, and taught them . . . —Matthew 5:1-2

Supplies

- Bible(s)
- sacred candle, matches or lighter
- sheet of paper
- crayons or colored pencils

 ## Welcoming God

Gather as a family and light a candle as a symbolic way of inviting God to join you during this time together. Sit quietly for a moment so that everyone has the opportunity to relax his or her body, mind, and spirit.

Sharing With God

Say: If there is anything weighing on our minds and making it difficult to focus, let us share it now and then let it go.

Enter a quiet time when family members can share. You might go first and set the example by sharing anything that is weighing on your own mind.

Listening for God

Say: Jesus spoke the Beatitudes, the Scripture we are going to read, to people who were poor, lonely, and felt that they did not belong. In the time of Jesus, many people believed that if anything went wrong in your life or you were not rich and famous, it was because God did not love you or was punishing you. Jesus taught us that God loves all of us—those who are rich and poor, popular and unpopular, outgoing and shy. God cares for and loves us all!

Read aloud Matthew 5:1-12. Take turns reading the Scripture, or have a different family member read the Scripture passage each week.

 Family Share and Reflection Time

Say: I am going to read the Scripture once again. This time listen for images in the Scripture that speak to you. After I am done, we all will draw the images that spoke to us on one sheet of paper to create a family picture of the Beatitudes.

Activity: Have family members draw their images on a single sheet of paper and talk about them as they work together. Then place the paper under your candle as a place mat for the next few weeks.

Discussion Questions:
- Was there one Beatitude that reminded you of yourself or someone you know?

- When things go wrong for you, is it hard to imagine that God still cares for you, or do you sometimes wonder if God is punishing you?
- Which Beatitude was your favorite?

 Asking God

Say: Let us pray together as a family . . .

> Let us share our prayers for the world—for our country and leaders, and for other countries and their leaders . . .
> Let us share our prayers for the church, ministers, and other spiritual leaders . . .
> Let us share our prayers for our friends, teachers, and others in our community . . .
> Let us share our prayers for family members and our own specific needs . . .

Use the space provided below to make note of family prayer requests. Take a few minutes to review requests from the previous week.

Prayer Requests:

_____
_____
_____
_____
_____

Offering Ourselves to God

Pray aloud together:

> God, we have read your Holy Word,
> We have prayed together,
> We have spent time with you,
> We have experienced your love for us,
> Now, we promise to love one another and others as you
>   love us.
> In the name of Christ. Amen.

Blessing One Another

Invite family members to bless one another. Some examples might be:

> "May God bless you, guide you, and be with you, today
>   and always. In the name of Christ, Amen."

> "I love you, and I ask God to bless you."

> "God loves you just the way you are, and so do I!"

Let Your Light Shine

You are the light of the world. . . .
Let your light shine before others, so that they may see
your good works and give glory to your Father in heaven.
—Matthew 5:14, 16

Supplies

- Bible(s)
- sacred candle, matches or lighter
- votive or other small candle and a jar that will fit over it

 ## Welcoming God

Gather as a family and light a candle as a symbolic way of inviting God to join you during this time together. Sit quietly for a moment so that everyone has the opportunity to relax his or her body, mind, and spirit.

Sharing With God

Say: If there is anything weighing on our minds and making it difficult to focus, let us share it now and then let it go.

Enter a quiet time when family members can share. You might go first and set the example by sharing anything that is weighing on your own mind.

Listening for God

Say: Jesus often used regular items such as bread, candles, mustard seeds, and even mountains to talk about God and how we should live. The image of light is one Jesus used many times. This Scripture tells us we should let our light shine.

Read aloud Matthew 5:13-20. Take turns reading the Scripture, or have a different family member read the Scripture passage each week.

 ## Family Share and Reflection Time

Say: Jesus told us to let our light shine and not to put it under a bushel or basket. We are going to do a science experiment that shows why Jesus told us to let our light shine and not to hide it.

Activity: Light the votive or small candle and place the jar over it. The lack of oxygen will cause the candle to go out. Do this several times, allowing each family member to try it once. Be careful, though, that the jar does not get too hot and burn anyone.

Discussion Questions:
- When we placed the candle under the jar, it went out. Do you think a similar thing can happen to us? If we put our light—the love of Jesus that is inside us—under a bushel, will it go out? In other words, if we stop being kind and loving as Jesus was, will we become mean and grumpy all the time? And if we are mean and grumpy all the time, do you think we will forget how to be like Jesus? Do you think

we need to practice being loving and kind so we won't forget how to be like Jesus? Why or why not?

- What light (gifts, talents, skills) do you have to share with those around you?
- How can we, as a family, help one another to "shine" and not let our lights go out? (Examples: be kind to one another, tell when we see a gift or talent in another family member, encourage one another)

 ## Asking God

Say: Let us pray together as a family . . .

Let us share our prayers for the world—for our country and leaders, and for other countries and their leaders . . .

Let us share our prayers for the church, ministers, and other spiritual leaders . . .

Let us share our prayers for our friends, teachers, and others in our community . . .

Let us share our prayers for family members and our own specific needs . . .

Use the space provided below to make note of family prayer requests. Take a few minutes to review requests from the previous week.

Prayer Requests:

_____

_____

_____

_____

_____

Offering Ourselves to God

Pray aloud together:

> God, we have read your Holy Word,
> We have prayed together,
> We have spent time with you,
> We have experienced your love for us,
> Now, we promise to love one another and others as you
>   love us.
> In the name of Christ. Amen.

Blessing One Another

Invite family members to bless one another. Some examples
might be:

> "May God bless you, guide you, and be with you, today
>   and always. In the name of Christ, Amen."

> "I love you, and I ask God to bless you."

> "God loves you just the way you are, and so do I!"

IN NEED OF HEALING

*All in the crowd were trying to touch him, for power
came out from him and healed all of them. —Luke 6:19*

Supplies
- Bible(s)
- sacred candle, matches or lighter
- ink pen
- adhesive bandage for each family member
- (Other options: object with a "crack" or "break" in it, sheet of paper with the word "PAIN" written on it, slips of paper or index cards)

Welcoming God

Gather as a family and light a candle as a symbolic way of inviting God to join you during this time together. Sit quietly for a moment so that everyone has the opportunity to relax his or her body, mind, and spirit.

Sharing With God

Say: If there is anything weighing on our minds and making it difficult to focus, let us share it now and then let it go.

Enter a quiet time when family members can share. You might go first and set the example by sharing anything that is weighing on your own mind.

Listening for God

Say: Jesus often healed people. This Scripture tells of many people coming to Jesus, asking to be healed, and receiving healing. Then Jesus reminds us that when we need healing, God loves and cares for us!

Read aloud Luke 6:17-26. Take turns reading the Scripture, or have a different family member read the Scripture passage each week.

 ## Family Share and Reflection Time

Say: Jesus healed people long ago, and we still ask for Jesus to heal us today. We can be healed physically, such as when we get better after a cold or when a broken arm heals. But we also can ask Jesus to heal us emotionally, such as when we have a broken heart or are struggling with a relationship.

Activity: Have each family member write on an adhesive bandage one hurt that he or she wants to ask Jesus to heal. The request can be for himself or herself, or on behalf of someone else who needs healing. One at a time, place the bandage on the family member while the entire family says, "We ask Jesus to heal this hurt!"

Older children and teens can do this activity as well. They will recognize the bandage as a symbol of pain, although they may not want the bandage to be placed on them. Another option is to use an object that has a "crack" or "break" in it, or a sheet of

paper with the word "PAIN" written on it. Or you simply might
have them write their requests on slips of paper or index cards.

Discussion Questions:
- Do you believe Jesus healed people in Bible times?
- Do you believe Jesus still heals people today?
- Do you think we should ask to be healed? Why or why not?

 ## Asking God

Say: Let us pray together as a family . . .

Let us share our prayers for the world—for our country
and leaders, and for other countries and their leaders . . .

Let us share our prayers for the church, ministers, and
other spiritual leaders . . .

Let us share our prayers for our friends, teachers, and
others in our community . . .

Let us share our prayers for family members and our own
specific needs . . .

Use the space provided below to make note of family prayer
requests. Take a few minutes to review requests from the previous week.

Prayer Requests:

_____

_____

_____

_____

_____

Offering Ourselves to God

Pray aloud together:

> God, we have read your Holy Word,
> We have prayed together,
> We have spent time with you,
> We have experienced your love for us,
> Now, we promise to love one another and others as you
> love us.
> In the name of Christ. Amen.

Blessing One Another

Invite family members to bless one another. Some examples might be:

> "May God bless you, guide you, and be with you, today
> and always. In the name of Christ, Amen."

> "I love you, and I ask God to bless you."

> "God loves you just the way you are, and so do I!"

LOVING OUR ENEMIES

"Love your enemies and pray for those who persecute you."
—Matthew 5:44

Supplies

- Bible(s)
- sacred candle, matches or lighter
- pens or pencils, small slip of paper for each family member

 ## Welcoming God

Gather as a family and light a candle as a symbolic way of inviting God to join you during this time together. Sit quietly for a moment so that everyone has the opportunity to relax his or her body, mind, and spirit.

Sharing With God

Say: If there is anything weighing on our minds and making it difficult to focus, let us share it now and then let it go.

Enter a quiet time when family members can share. You might go first and set the example by sharing anything that is weighing on your own mind.

Listening for God

Say: Jesus taught us a lot about how to be loving. He reminded us that it is easy to love our friends, but it is hard to love our enemies. Jesus reminds us that we need to love everyone.

Read aloud Matthew 5:38-48. Take turns reading the Scripture, or have a different family member read the Scripture passage each week.

 ## Family Share and Reflection Time

Say: I am going to give each of us a slip of paper. It is difficult to admit that we have enemies, but we all do. I am going to give each of us a slip of paper. On this slip of paper, you are to write the name of someone you find difficult to love—or you can name a situation that you do not like. Then, one at a time, we will place the slips of paper by the candle and, if we want to, share about what we have written. You do not have to share. Then we will pray silently for our enemies.

Activity: Have each family member reflect and write down the name of an enemy—or a situation he or she does not like. If children cannot write yet, they can draw a picture of a person or situation. Then, one by one, place the slips of paper by the candle, sharing as you are willing. Pray silently for a few moments for the named persons and situations. After the time together, tear up the slips of paper and throw them away for privacy and confidentiality.

Discussion Questions:

- Was it difficult or easy to admit you have enemies?
- Do you feel any different about the person/situation after you prayed for him or her/it?
- Do you think you are anyone's enemy? Is there anything you can do to change the situation?

 ## Asking God

Say: Let us pray together as a family . . .

Let us share our prayers for the world—for our country and leaders, and for other countries and their leaders . . .

Let us share our prayers for the church, ministers, and other spiritual leaders . . .

Let us share our prayers for our friends, teachers, and others in our community . . .

Let us share our prayers for family members and our own specific needs . . .

Use the space provided below to make note of family prayer requests. Take a few minutes to review requests from the previous week.

Prayer Requests:

_____

_____

_____

_____

_____

Offering Ourselves to God

Pray aloud together:

> God, we have read your Holy Word,
> We have prayed together,
> We have spent time with you,
> We have experienced your love for us,
> Now, we promise to love one another and others as you
>   love us.
> In the name of Christ. Amen.

Blessing One Another

Invite family members to bless one another. Some examples might be:

> "May God bless you, guide you, and be with you, today and always. In the name of Christ, Amen."

> "I love you, and I ask God to bless you."

> "God loves you just the way you are, and so do I!"

JESUS TEACHES US A NEW WAY

Jesus went out again beside the sea; the whole crowd gathered around him, and he taught them. —Mark 2:13

Supplies
- Bible(s)
- sacred candle, matches or lighter
- paper or plastic cup with some vinegar in it
- large bowl
- 3 tablespoons baking soda

 ## Welcoming God

Gather as a family and light a candle as a symbolic way of inviting God to join you during this time together. Sit quietly for a moment so that everyone has the opportunity to relax his or her body, mind, and spirit.

Sharing With God

Say: If there is anything weighing on our minds and making it difficult to focus, let us share it now and then let it go.

Enter a quiet time when family members can share. You might go first and set the example by sharing anything that is weighing on your own mind.

Listening for God

Say: Jesus did things very differently than the other religious leaders. He did things his own way and taught people new ideas, and some people became angry because of this.

Read aloud Mark 2:13-22. Take turns reading the Scripture, or have a different family member read the Scripture passage each week.

 Family Share and Reflection Time

Say: Jesus loved people that others did not love. Jesus taught people that they had to change the old ways of doing things and do things a new way. Jesus shook things up wherever he went. We are going to do a science experiment that will demonstrate what happens when we follow Jesus: everything changes!

Activity: Place some vinegar in a cup and place the cup inside a bowl. Explain that the cup of vinegar is like the old way people used to do things. It just sits still and stays the same. When Jesus came along, everything changed. Sprinkle the baking soda into the cup and watch as the vinegar bubbles and overflows. This can be a lot of fun for kids of all ages. Let older children and teens conduct the experiment from beginning to end. Ask them what they think will happen *before* adding the baking soda to the vinegar. Invite younger children to participate by sprinkling the baking soda, repeating the experiment several times so that each child has a turn.

Discussion Questions:

- Many of the people who heard Jesus did not want to change. Is change easy or difficult for you?
- Jesus makes life different! How has being a Christian changed your life? How do you think you are different because you are a Christian?

 ## Asking God

Say: Let us pray together as a family . . .

> Let us share our prayers for the world—for our country and leaders, and for other countries and their leaders . . .
>
> Let us share our prayers for the church, ministers, and other spiritual leaders . . .
>
> Let us share our prayers for our friends, teachers, and others in our community . . .
>
> Let us share our prayers for family members and our own specific needs . . .

Use the space provided below to make note of family prayer requests. Take a few minutes to review requests from the previous week.

Prayer Requests:

_____

_____

_____

_____

_____

Offering Ourselves to God

Pray aloud together:

>God, we have read your Holy Word,
>We have prayed together,
>We have spent time with you,
>We have experienced your love for us,
>Now, we promise to love one another and others as you
>   love us.
>In the name of Christ. Amen.

Blessing One Another

Invite family members to bless one another. Some examples
might be:

>"May God bless you, guide you, and be with you, today
>   and always. In the name of Christ, Amen."

>"I love you, and I ask God to bless you."

>"God loves you just the way you are, and so do I!"

TIME ON THE MOUNTAIN

Now about eight days after these sayings Jesus took with him Peter and John and James, and went up on the mountain to pray.
—Luke 9:28

Supplies
- Bible(s)
- sacred candle, matches or lighter
- large blanket or sheet

 ## Welcoming God

Gather as a family and light a candle as a symbolic way of inviting God to join you during this time together. Sit quietly for a moment so that everyone has the opportunity to relax his or her body, mind, and spirit.

Sharing With God

Say: If there is anything weighing on our minds and making it difficult to focus, let us share it now and then let it go.

Enter a quiet time when family members can share. You might go first and set the example by sharing anything that is weighing on your own mind.

Listening for God

Say: This story is about a time when Jesus and three of his friends went up on a mountain, and while they were there they were joined by some prophets who had died, Elijah and Moses.

Read aloud Luke 9:28-36. Take turns reading the Scripture, or have a different family member read the Scripture passage each week.

Family Share and Reflection Time

Say: When they reached the top of the mountain, it felt so wonderful that one of Jesus' friends wanted to build tents and stay for a while. But they could not stay on the mountain. They had to get back to the real world. Sometimes it is fun to escape and get away from it all.

Activity: Make a tent by placing a blanket or sheet over a table or chairs. Have your entire family sit under it, hold hands, and listen to the quiet of the moment. Really try and enjoy the time away from the world. Giggling is okay as well! If you do not have younger children, you might choose instead to find a quiet, peaceful place within or outside your home. Turn off all electronic devices and sit in silence for a few moments.

Discussion Questions:
- This story happened right before Jesus faced his last days before his death. He needed to get away and be refreshed. What is stressing you out right now?

- Where and how do you get away and refresh your body and soul?
- Are there things you need to do regularly to become rested and refreshed?

 Asking God

Say: Let us pray together as a family . . .

Let us share our prayers for the world—for our country and leaders, and for other countries and their leaders . . .

Let us share our prayers for the church, ministers, and other spiritual leaders . . .

Let us share our prayers for our friends, teachers, and others in our community . . .

Let us share our prayers for family members and our own specific needs . . .

Use the space provided below to make note of family prayer requests. Take a few minutes to review requests from the previous week.

Prayer Requests:

_____

_____

_____

_____

_____

Offering Ourselves to God

Pray aloud together:

God, we have read your Holy Word,
We have prayed together,
We have spent time with you,
We have experienced your love for us,
Now, we promise to love one another and others as you
    love us.
In the name of Christ. Amen.

Blessing One Another

Invite family members to bless one another. Some examples
might be:

"May God bless you, guide you, and be with you, today
    and always. In the name of Christ, Amen."

"I love you, and I ask God to bless you."

"God loves you just the way you are, and so do I!"

THE TEMPTATION OF JESUS

*Then Jesus was led up by the Spirit into the wilderness
to be tempted by the devil. —Matthew 4:1*

Supplies
- Bible(s)
- sacred candle, matches or lighter
- piece of fresh fruit
- candy bar

 ## Welcoming God

Gather as a family and light a candle as a symbolic way of inviting God to join you during this time together. Sit quietly for a moment so that everyone has the opportunity to relax his or her body, mind, and spirit.

Sharing With God

Say: If there is anything weighing on our minds and making it difficult to focus, let us share it now and then let it go.

Enter a quiet time when family members can share. You might go first and set the example by sharing anything that is weighing on your own mind.

Listening for God

Say: This is the first week of Lent. Lent, the forty days before Easter, is a time when we try to intentionally grow closer to Jesus. Our Scripture today is the story of Jesus being tempted as he began his ministry.

Read aloud Matthew 4:1-11. Take turns reading the Scripture, or have a different family member read the Scripture passage each week.

 ## Family Share and Reflection Time

Say: Temptation is when we want to do something we shouldn't. Even Jesus was tempted sometimes. This piece of fruit represents good and healthy choices we have, and this candy bar reminds us that whenever we have a choice, temptation is close by.

Activity: Pass the candy bar around and have each person share something that tempts him or her. Then pass the fruit around, and as each person holds it, have your family say in unison, "We believe in you, (name of person), and your ability to resist temptation."

Discussion Questions:
- Do you think Jesus was really tempted? Why or why not?
- When you are tempted to do something you know you shouldn't do, what are some things you might try before you act on your desire?
- If you do make a mistake, do you think you would be forgiven by God and by our family?

 **Asking God**

Say: Let us pray together as a family . . .

Let us share our prayers for the world—for our country and leaders, and for other countries and their leaders . . .

Let us share our prayers for the church, ministers, and other spiritual leaders . . .

Let us share our prayers for our friends, teachers, and others in our community . . .

Let us share our prayers for family members and our own specific needs . . .

Use the space provided below to make note of family prayer requests. Take a few minutes to review requests from the previous week.

Prayer Requests:

_____

_____

_____

_____

_____

Offering Ourselves to God

Pray aloud together:

God, we have read your Holy Word,
We have prayed together,
We have spent time with you,
We have experienced your love for us,

Now, we promise to love one another and others as you love us.
In the name of Christ. Amen.

Blessing One Another

Invite family members to bless one another. Some examples might be:

"May God bless you, guide you, and be with you, today and always. In the name of Christ, Amen."

"I love you, and I ask God to bless you."

"God loves you just the way you are, and so do I!"

GOD'S LOVE FOR US

"For God so loved the world that he gave his one and only Son, that whoever believes in him shall not perish but have eternal life."
—John 3:16 (NIV)

Supplies
- Bible(s)
- sacred candle, matches or lighter
- *optional for older children, teens:* paper, pens, markers or colored pencils

 ## Welcoming God

Gather as a family and light a candle as a symbolic way of inviting God to join you during this time together. Sit quietly for a moment so that everyone has the opportunity to relax his or her body, mind, and spirit.

Sharing With God

Say: If there is anything weighing on our minds and making it difficult to focus, let us share it now and then let it go.

Enter a quiet time when family members can share. You might go first and set the example by sharing anything that is weighing on your own mind.

Listening for God

Say: This is the second week of Lent. As we get ready for Easter, it is a good time to be reminded of just how much God loves us! This Scripture passage is sometimes called the heart of the gospel because it so beautifully describes God's love.

Read aloud John 3:16-17. Take turns reading the Scripture, or have a different family member read the Scripture passage each week.

 Family Share and Reflection Time

Say: This Scripture is so beautiful. It is a good one to memorize. Let's work on the first verse, John 3:16, today.

Activity: Try to memorize verse 16 of the Scripture passage as a family. Say it several times together. Sometimes making up motions to go along with the Scripture or even a song will help you to remember it. For older children and teens who already know the Scripture, invite them to write the verse in their own words or to write a poem or story illustrating the love of God for us.

Discussion Questions:
- Do you ever feel God's love? When?
- What do you think eternal life will be like? What do you think heaven will be like?
- Do you think God loves everyone in the world or just certain people? Why?

 **Asking God**

Say: Let us pray together as a family . . .

> Let us share our prayers for the world—for our country and leaders, and for other countries and their leaders . . .
>
> Let us share our prayers for the church, ministers, and other spiritual leaders . . .
>
> Let us share our prayers for our friends, teachers, and others in our community . . .
>
> Let us share our prayers for family members and our own specific needs . . .

Use the space provided below to make note of family prayer requests. Take a few minutes to review requests from the previous week.

Prayer Requests:

_____

_____

_____

_____

_____

Offering Ourselves to God

Pray aloud together:

> God, we have read your Holy Word,
> We have prayed together,
> We have spent time with you,
> We have experienced your love for us,

Now, we promise to love one another and others as you love us.

In the name of Christ. Amen.

Blessing One Another

Invite family members to bless one another. Some examples might be:

"May God bless you, guide you, and be with you, today and always. In the name of Christ, Amen."

"I love you, and I ask God to bless you."

"God loves you just the way you are, and so do I!"

JESUS GETS ANGRY

[Jesus] made a whip out of cords, and drove all from the temple area, both sheep and cattle; he scattered the coins of the money changers and overturned their tables.
—John 2:15 (NIV)

Supplies
- Bible(s)
- sacred candle, matches or lighter
- sheet of paper for each family member (or a pillow; or a board, nails, and hammer)

 ## Welcoming God

Gather as a family and light a candle as a symbolic way of inviting God to join you during this time together. Sit quietly for a moment so that everyone has the opportunity to relax his or her body, mind, and spirit.

Sharing With God

Say: If there is anything weighing on our minds and making it difficult to focus, let us share it now and then let it go.

Enter a quiet time when family members can share. You might go first and set the example by sharing anything that is weighing on your own mind.

Listening for God

Say: This is the third week of Lent. In our Scripture reading, Jesus has come to Jerusalem for a special celebration called Passover. But on his way, he discovers that people are selling things in the Temple and taking money from the poor. These people were doing bad things in God's house, and it made Jesus become angry.

Read aloud John 2:13-22. Take turns reading the Scripture, or have a different family member read the Scripture passage each week.

Family Share and Reflection Time

Say: When some people read this story, they are surprised to learn that Jesus got angry. Some people think Jesus never got angry; but he was completely human, and all people get angry. Jesus had a good reason to be angry because the people were turning God's house, which was supposed to be a house of prayer, into a marketplace. He had what is called righteous anger, and he took actions to demonstrate that what the people were doing was wrong.

We have to be careful how we handle anger. Sometimes we have a good reason to be angry, like Jesus, and sometimes we do not. But we always need to respond to our anger in appropriate ways without hurting others. We need to learn how to "let out" our anger in positive ways, such as drawing a picture, talking to someone, or running really fast until we have let out all our anger.

Activity: Give each family member a blank sheet of paper and ask everyone to think of something that makes him or her really angry. One at a time, have family members share the things that make them angry. As each person shares, have him or her tear the paper as a way of letting the anger out. Or, invite family members to punch a pillow or hammer a nail into a board. Be as creative as you like. Make this a fun way to remind children and teens that there are non-hurtful ways to express our anger.

Discussion Questions:

- Does it surprise you that Jesus got angry? Why or why not?
- What are some good ways to let your anger out?
- What are some ways you might peacefully confront or talk to someone who has hurt you or others?

 Asking God

Say: Let us pray together as a family . . .

> Let us share our prayers for the world—for our country and leaders, and for other countries and their leaders . . .
>
> Let us share our prayers for the church, ministers, and other spiritual leaders . . .
>
> Let us share our prayers for our friends, teachers, and others in our community . . .
>
> Let us share our prayers for family members and our own specific needs . . .

Use the space provided on the next page to make note of family prayer requests. Take a few minutes to review requests from the previous week.

Prayer Requests:

_____

_____

_____

_____

_____

Offering Ourselves to God

Pray aloud together:

> God, we have read your Holy Word,
> We have prayed together,
> We have spent time with you,
> We have experienced your love for us,
> Now, we promise to love one another and others as you
>   love us.
> In the name of Christ. Amen.

Blessing One Another

Invite family members to bless one another. Some examples
might be:

> "May God bless you, guide you, and be with you, today
>   and always. In the name of Christ, Amen."

> "I love you, and I ask God to bless you."

> "God loves you just the way you are, and so do I!"

ARE WE GROWING CLOSER TO JESUS?

Light has come into the world, but men loved darkness instead of light because their deeds were evil. —John 3:19 (NIV)

Supplies

- Bible(s)
- sacred candle, matches or lighter
- small bowl filled with water
- pepper
- dish soap

 ## Welcoming God

Gather as a family and light a candle as a symbolic way of inviting God to join you during this time together. Sit quietly for a moment so that everyone has the opportunity to relax his or her body, mind, and spirit.

Sharing With God

Say: If there is anything weighing on our minds and making it difficult to focus, let us share it now and then let it go.

Enter a quiet time when family members can share. You might go first and set the example by sharing anything that is weighing on your own mind.

Listening for God

Say: Our Scripture today is a lesson Jesus gave as he explained how some people grow closer to him while others reject him and run away from his teachings and lessons. As we read the Scripture, listen for the verse we memorized two weeks ago (John 3:16). As we move through Lent, it is important to ask ourselves if we are growing closer to Jesus or running away from him.

Read aloud John 3:14-21. Take turns reading the Scripture, or have a different family member read the Scripture passage each week.

 Family Share and Reflection Time

Say: Jesus was so good and so loving. It is difficult to think that some people did not love him or want to listen to him. This experiment will demonstrate how some people ran from Jesus and refused to listen to him. Let's pretend that the pepper flakes are those people and the dish soap is the light of Jesus.

(Note: With older children and teens, you might do the activity first and have them explain how this experiment illustrates the lesson of the Scripture.)

Activity: Fill the bowl with tap water. Cover the surface of the water with pepper. Place one drop of dish soap in the middle of the bowl and watch the pepper move away.

Discussion Questions:
- Why do you think some people did not follow Jesus?

- Do you know anyone who does not love or follow Jesus? Is there anything you can do to show this person the love of Jesus?
- Are you ever tempted to run away from Jesus and not do the things he wants you to do? Why?
- Are you growing closer to Jesus? What might help you to grow closer to him?

 Asking God

Say: Let us pray together as a family . . .

Let us share our prayers for the world—for our country and leaders, and for other countries and their leaders . . .

Let us share our prayers for the church, ministers, and other spiritual leaders . . .

Let us share our prayers for our friends, teachers, and others in our community . . .

Let us share our prayers for family members and our own specific needs . . .

Use the space provided below to make note of family prayer requests. Take a few minutes to review requests from the previous week.

Prayer Requests:

_____

_____

_____

_____

_____

Offering Ourselves to God

Pray aloud together:

> God, we have read your Holy Word,
> We have prayed together,
> We have spent time with you,
> We have experienced your love for us,
> Now, we promise to love one another and others as you
>   love us.
> In the name of Christ. Amen.

Blessing One Another

Invite family members to bless one another. Some examples might be:

> "May God bless you, guide you, and be with you, today and always. In the name of Christ, Amen."

> "I love you, and I ask God to bless you."

> "God loves you just the way you are, and so do I!"

WASHING ONE ANOTHER'S FEET

Mary took a pound of costly perfume made of pure nard, anointed Jesus' feet, and wiped them with her hair. —John 12:3

Supplies
- Bible(s)
- sacred candle, matches or lighter
- large dish or pan of warm water
- soap
- towel

 ## Welcoming God

Gather as a family and light a candle as a symbolic way of inviting God to join you during this time together. Sit quietly for a moment so that everyone has the opportunity to relax his or her body, mind, and spirit.

Sharing With God

Say: If there is anything weighing on our minds and making it difficult to focus, let us share it now and then let it go.

Enter a quiet time when family members can share. You might go first and set the example by sharing anything that is weighing on your own mind.

Listening for God

Say: On this fifth week of Lent, we move closer in our story toward the death of Jesus. Before he ate his last supper and prayed in the garden and was arrested, beaten, and killed, a woman did a very kind thing for him. She poured expensive perfume on his feet and wiped them with her hair.

Read aloud John 12:1-8. Take turns reading the Scripture, or have a different family member read the Scripture passage each week.

Family Share and Reflection Time

Say: In the time of Jesus, washing someone's feet was a way of showing how much you cared for and loved the person. We are going to wash one another's feet in memory of this Scripture story and also to show love and care to one another.

Activity: Take turns washing one another's feet. If you have time, have each family member wash the feet of everyone else. Otherwise, determine who will wash whose feet. Try not to talk during this activity but let your loving actions say everything that needs to be said.

Discussion Questions:
- How did it feel to have your feet washed?
- How did it feel to wash another person's feet?

- What are some ways we show our love for one another?
- Could we do a better job of showing our love to one another? How?

 Asking God

Say: Let us pray together as a family . . .

Let us share our prayers for the world—for our country and leaders, and for other countries and their leaders . . .

Let us share our prayers for the church, ministers, and other spiritual leaders . . .

Let us share our prayers for our friends, teachers, and others in our community . . .

Let us share our prayers for family members and our own specific needs . . .

Use the space provided below to make note of family prayer requests. Take a few minutes to review requests from the previous week.

Prayer Requests:

_____

_____

_____

_____

_____

Offering Ourselves to God

Pray aloud together:

> God, we have read your Holy Word,
> We have prayed together,
> We have spent time with you,
> We have experienced your love for us,
> Now, we promise to love one another and others as you
> love us.
> In the name of Christ. Amen.

Blessing One Another

Invite family members to bless one another. Some examples
might be:

> "May God bless you, guide you, and be with you, today
> and always. In the name of Christ, Amen."

> "I love you, and I ask God to bless you."

> "God loves you just the way you are, and so do I!"

JESUS' DEATH

They brought Jesus to the place called Golgotha
(which means the place of a skull). . . . And they crucified him.
—Mark 15:22, 24

Supplies

- Bible(s)
- sacred candle, matches or lighter
- cup of warm water, salt

 ## Welcoming God

Gather as a family and light a candle as a symbolic way of inviting God to join you during this time together. Sit quietly for a moment so that everyone has the opportunity to relax his or her body, mind, and spirit.

Sharing With God

Say: If there is anything weighing on our minds and making it difficult to focus, let us share it now and then let it go.

Enter a quiet time when family members can share. You might go first and set the example by sharing anything that is weighing on your own mind.

Listening for God

Say: This is the last week of Lent. During this week, Jesus entered Jerusalem on a donkey while people waved palm branches. But then things began to get very sad. Jesus ate his last supper with his disciples and friends; he prayed in the garden of Gethsemane; one of his friends betrayed him; and he was arrested, beaten, and crucified on a cross. This Scripture tells about the unfair trial of Jesus and his death. It is a very, very sad story; but remember, it gets happy again on Easter. Today, though, is sad!

Read aloud Mark 15:1-47. Take turns reading the Scripture, or have a different family member read the Scripture passage each week.

 ## Family Share and Reflection Time

Say: This is the saddest story in the entire Bible! It also is a hard story to understand because Jesus, who was loving, kind, and wonderful, was killed. Let us taste the sadness of this story and then sit quietly thinking about it.

Activity: Dissolve some salt in a cup of warm water. Pass around the cup of salty water, inviting each person to dip a finger into it and taste the sad tears that have been shed by so many Christians over the death of Jesus.

Discussion Questions:

- What feelings did you experience while the story was read and while you reflected on it?

- Why do you think Jesus was killed? Do you think it was part of God's plan? Do you think anything could have been done to prevent his death?
- Are you excited for Easter to come and shatter this sadness?
- (For older children and teens) As you reflect on Jesus' crucifixion, what thoughts and feelings do you have? What meaning or significance would Jesus' death have apart from his resurrection on Easter morning?

 ## Asking God

Say: Let us pray together as a family . . .

Let us share our prayers for the world—for our country and leaders, and for other countries and their leaders . . .

Let us share our prayers for the church, ministers, and other spiritual leaders . . .

Let us share our prayers for our friends, teachers, and others in our community . . .

Let us share our prayers for family members and our own specific needs . . .

Use the space provided below to make note of family prayer requests. Take a few minutes to review requests from the previous week.

Prayer Requests:

_____

_____

_____

_____

_____

Offering Ourselves to God

Pray aloud together:

> God, we have read your Holy Word,
> We have prayed together,
> We have spent time with you,
> We have experienced your love for us,
> Now, we promise to love one another and others as you
> love us.
> In the name of Christ. Amen.

Blessing One Another

Invite family members to bless one another. Some examples might be:

> "May God bless you, guide you, and be with you, today
> and always. In the name of Christ, Amen."

> "I love you, and I ask God to bless you."

> "God loves you just the way you are, and so do I!"

HE HAS RISEN

As they entered the tomb, they saw a young man dressed in a white robe, sitting on the right side; and they were alarmed. But he said to them, "Do not be alarmed; you are looking for Jesus of Nazareth, who was crucified. He has been raised; he is not here. Look, there is the place they laid him." —Mark 16:5-6

Supplies
- Bible(s)
- sacred candle, matches or lighter
- small bowl
- a raw egg and straight pin for each family member

 ## Welcoming God

Gather as a family and light a candle as a symbolic way of inviting God to join you during this time together. Sit quietly for a moment so that everyone has the opportunity to relax his or her body, mind, and spirit.

Sharing With God

Say: If there is anything weighing on our minds and making it difficult to focus, let us share it now and then let it go.

Enter a quiet time when family members can share. You might go first and set the example by sharing anything that is weighing on your own mind.

Listening for God

Say: On the day Jesus died, his friends took him off the cross and laid him in the tomb. On Easter morning, when they went to the grave, his body was gone. Jesus had risen from the dead. His death is the saddest story in the Bible, but his resurrection is the happiest story ever!

Read aloud Mark 16:1-8. Take turns reading the Scripture, or have a different family member read the Scripture passage each week.

Family Share and Reflection Time

Say: Jesus' friends were surprised to find the tomb was empty. We are going to make empty tombs out of eggs and retell the story using our own tombs.

Activity: Make two holes in each egg using a straight pin, one on top and one on bottom, and have each family member blow the insides out into a bowl. This should be fun, so make the holes large enough so that it is not frustrating. After blowing the eggs, have each family member tell the story of Christ's resurrection in his or her own words. When the person gets to the part about the empty tomb, have him or her crack open the empty egg. If family members tire of hearing the story, remind them that this is the greatest story of all time and needs to be heard time and time again!

Discussion Questions:

- God surprised the whole world with the resurrection of Jesus. Has God ever surprised you? How?

- How do you think Jesus' friends felt when they found the tomb empty?
- How does knowing that Jesus rose from dead make you feel?
- Where do you need a miracle in your own life?

 Asking God

Say: Let us pray together as a family . . .

Let us share our prayers for the world—for our country and leaders, and for other countries and their leaders . . .

Let us share our prayers for the church, ministers, and other spiritual leaders . . .

Let us share our prayers for our friends, teachers, and others in our community . . .

Let us share our prayers for family members and our own specific needs . . .

Use the space provided below to make note of family prayer requests. Take a few minutes to review requests from the previous week.

Prayer Requests:

_____

_____

_____

_____

_____

Offering Ourselves to God

Pray aloud together:

> God, we have read your Holy Word,
> We have prayed together,
> We have spent time with you,
> We have experienced your love for us,
> Now, we promise to love one another and others as you
>   love us.
> In the name of Christ. Amen.

Blessing One Another

Invite family members to bless one another. Some examples might be:

> "May God bless you, guide you, and be with you, today
>   and always. In the name of Christ, Amen."

> "I love you, and I ask God to bless you."

> "God loves you just the way you are, and so do I!"

THE PEACE OF JESUS

When it was evening on that day, the first day of the week, and the doors of the house where the disciples had met were locked for fear of the Jews, Jesus came and stood among them and said, "Peace be with you." —John 20:19

Supplies

- Bible(s)
- sacred candle, matches or lighter
- sheet of paper
- pen

 ## Welcoming God

Gather as a family and light a candle as a symbolic way of inviting God to join you during this time together. Sit quietly for a moment so that everyone has the opportunity to relax his or her body, mind, and spirit.

Sharing With God

Say: If there is anything weighing on our minds and making it difficult to focus, let us share it now and then let it go.

Enter a quiet time when family members can share. You might go first and set the example by sharing anything that is weighing on your own mind.

Listening for God

Say: On Easter, Jesus arose from the dead. Then for several days he visited his followers and friends. He came to their homes, ate with them, and even went fishing with them! This is a story of Jesus' visit to his disciples.

Read aloud John 20:19-23. Take turns reading the Scripture, or have a different family member read the Scripture passage each week.

 Family Share and Reflection Time

Say: The followers were shaken and upset after Jesus died, and so they were together in one place because they were afraid. Jesus appeared and said, "Peace be with you!" Then he told them that from this time forward, they were to become peacemakers. This activity will help us to compare some peaceful and non-peaceful responses.

Activity: Fold the sheet of paper in half lengthwise, creating two columns. Label the left side "Non-peaceful" and the right side "Peaceful." As a family, think of situations when a quick response is needed, such as when someone is bullying you, pressuring you to do something you know you shouldn't do, or yelling at you unfairly. Together decide what a non-peaceful response and a peaceful response might be; write these on the appropriate sides of the paper. After doing several scenarios, tear the paper in half along the fold line. Throw the non-peaceful responses in the trash. Place the peaceful responses on the refrigerator as a reminder that we are called to be peacemakers!

Discussion Questions:

- When was the last time you had to respond to a difficult situation? Did you respond peacefully or non-peacefully?
- Do we tend to respond to other members in our family peacefully or non-peacefully? Share some examples.
- What are some ways we could be kinder when responding to one another?

 Asking God

Say: Let us pray together as a family . . .

Let us share our prayers for the world—for our country and leaders, and for other countries and their leaders . . .

Let us share our prayers for the church, ministers, and other spiritual leaders . . .

Let us share our prayers for our friends, teachers, and others in our community . . .

Let us share our prayers for family members and our own specific needs . . .

Use the space provided below to make note of family prayer requests. Take a few minutes to review requests from the previous week.

Prayer Requests:

_____

_____

_____

_____

_____

Offering Ourselves to God

Pray aloud together:

> God, we have read your Holy Word,
> We have prayed together,
> We have spent time with you,
> We have experienced your love for us,
> Now, we promise to love one another and others as you
> love us.
> In the name of Christ. Amen.

Blessing One Another

Invite family members to bless one another. Some examples might be:

> "May God bless you, guide you, and be with you, today and always. In the name of Christ, Amen."

> "I love you, and I ask God to bless you."

> "God loves you just the way you are, and so do I!"

SHARING THE BREAD OF JESUS

*While in their joy they were disbelieving and still wondering, he
said to them, "Have you anything here to eat?" They gave him a
piece of broiled fish, and he took it and ate in their presence.*
—Luke 24:41-43

Supplies
- Bible(s)
- sacred candle, matches or lighter
- can of biscuits
- cookie sheet
- preheated oven

 ## Welcoming God

Gather as a family and light a candle as a symbolic way of inviting God to join you during this time together. Sit quietly for a
moment so that everyone has the opportunity to relax his or her
body, mind, and spirit.

Sharing With God

Say: If there is anything weighing on our minds and making it
difficult to focus, let us share it now and then let it go.

Enter a quiet time when family members can share. You might
go first and set the example by sharing anything that is weighing on your own mind.

Listening for God

Say: This is another story of a time when Jesus appeared to his friends after he rose from the dead. Jesus asked them if they had anything to eat and they gave him fish. They were happy Jesus was with them.

Read aloud Luke 24:36b-48. Take turns reading the Scripture, or have a different family member read the Scripture passage each week.

 ## Family Share and Reflection Time

Say: In this story, Jesus ate fish. Early Christians used the fish as a symbol to let others know they were Christians. There are many symbols we can make that remind us we are Christians. The fish, a cross, and the Communion chalice are all symbols the church has used. But anything that reminds you of God's love and care for us can be a symbol.

Activity: Have each family member think of a symbol of God's love, such as a cross, a heart, friends hugging, a rainbow, a Communion chalice, and so on. Then have each person make a symbol out of biscuit dough and bake it. When the bread is done, invite each family member to show and tell about the symbol he or she made. Then break the bread and share it in remembrance of Jesus. Enjoy the sacred meal.

Discussion Questions:
- Why do you think symbols are so important and special?
- Do you see any symbols of God's love in our home?

- We used bread as a way of sharing our symbols. Jesus used bread at his last supper. Do you think using bread could be a symbol of anything?
- Why do you think Jesus used symbols, such bread or juice or mustard seeds, so often when he taught people?

 Asking God

Say: Let us pray together as a family . . .

Let us share our prayers for the world—for our country and leaders, and for other countries and their leaders . . .

Let us share our prayers for the church, ministers, and other spiritual leaders . . .

Let us share our prayers for our friends, teachers, and others in our community . . .

Let us share our prayers for family members and our own specific needs . . .

Use the space provided below to make note of family prayer requests. Take a few minutes to review requests from the previous week.

Prayer Requests:

_____

_____

_____

_____

_____

Offering Ourselves to God

Pray aloud together:

> God, we have read your Holy Word,
> We have prayed together,
> We have spent time with you,
> We have experienced your love for us,
> Now, we promise to love one another and others as you
>   love us.
> In the name of Christ. Amen.

Blessing One Another

Invite family members to bless one another. Some examples
might be:

> "May God bless you, guide you, and be with you, today
>   and always. In the name of Christ, Amen."

> "I love you, and I ask God to bless you."

> "God loves you just the way you are, and so do I!"

THE GOOD SHEPHERD

He calls his own sheep by name and leads them out. . . .
and the sheep follow him because they know his voice.
—John 10:3b-4

Supplies
- Bible(s)
- sacred candle, matches or lighter
- *optional for older children, teens:* recordings of various songs

Welcoming God

Gather as a family and light a candle as a symbolic way of inviting God to join you during this time together. Sit quietly for a moment so that everyone has the opportunity to relax his or her body, mind, and spirit.

Sharing With God

Say: If there is anything weighing on our minds and making it difficult to focus, let us share it now and then let it go.

Enter a quiet time when family members can share. You might go first and set the example by sharing anything that is weighing on your own mind.

Listening for God

Say: In this story Jesus compares himself to a good shepherd and us, his followers, to sheep. He tells us that we need to listen to him and learn his voice so we can follow him at all times.

Read aloud John 10:1-6. Take turns reading the Scripture, or have a different family member read the Scripture passage each week.

Family Share and Reflection Time

Say: To follow Jesus, we must listen for his voice calling us to follow him. We are going to play a game that will help us to realize that we must listen closely to Jesus' voice.

Activity: If you have younger children, play hide and seek. One member of the family is "It" and hides. Then "It" calls out repeatedly, "Little sheep, I am calling!" Family members listen for "Its" voice until they find him or her. Play this game several times, allowing different family members to be "It." Choose fun hiding places such as under a bed, in a closet, or even outside the house.

If you have older children or teens, you might play "name that artist" instead. Play songs by singers or groups that family members are familiar with, as well as some they will not recognize. The first person to name the correct artist each time gets one point. Whoever has the most points after a period of time is the winner.

Whichever game you play, point out that we must listen closely to Jesus' voice if we are to follow him.

Discussion Questions:

- Was it easy or difficult to find the person who was hiding (or to identify the correct artist)? Why?
- How does Jesus call us today?
- How can we listen to Jesus' voice? What are some ways we can hear Jesus?
- What helped you to find the person who was hiding (or to identify the artist)? Can we use any of those same techniques when listening for our Shepherd, Jesus? How?

 Asking God

Say: Let us pray together as a family . . .

Let us share our prayers for the world—for our country and leaders, and for other countries and their leaders . . .

Let us share our prayers for the church, ministers, and other spiritual leaders . . .

Let us share our prayers for our friends, teachers, and others in our community . . .

Let us share our prayers for family members and our own specific needs . . .

Use the space provided on the next page to make note of family prayer requests. Take a few minutes to review requests from the previous week.

Prayer Requests:

_____

_____

_____

_____

_____

Offering Ourselves to God

Pray aloud together:

God, we have read your Holy Word,
We have prayed together,
We have spent time with you,
We have experienced your love for us,
Now, we promise to love one another and others as you
   love us.
In the name of Christ. Amen.

Blessing One Another

Invite family members to bless one another. Some examples
might be:

"May God bless you, guide you, and be with you, today
   and always. In the name of Christ, Amen."

"I love you, and I ask God to bless you."

"God loves you just the way you are, and so do I!"

THE VINE OF GOD

I am the vine, you are the branches. —John 15:5

Supplies

- Bible(s)
- sacred candle, matches or lighter
- sheet of paper
- crayons or markers or colored pencils

 ## Welcoming God

Gather as a family and light a candle as a symbolic way of inviting God to join you during this time together. Sit quietly for a moment so that everyone has the opportunity to relax his or her body, mind, and spirit.

Sharing With God

Say: If there is anything weighing on our minds and making it difficult to focus, let us share it now and then let it go.

Enter a quiet time when family members can share. You might go first and set the example by sharing anything that is weighing on your own mind.

 ## Listening for God

Say: In this Scripture, Jesus tells us that he is the vine and from him everything grows.

Read aloud John 15:1-8. Take turns reading the Scripture, or have a different family member read the Scripture passage each week.

Family Share and Reflection Time

Say: Jesus describes himself as the vine from which we all grow. We are going to draw our family vine coming from the vine of Jesus.

Activity: As a family, draw a "family vine" (similar to a family tree but more vine-like). Make Jesus the center vine and family members—both immediate and extended—the smaller branches extending from the vine.

Discussion Questions:

- Who on our family vine do you feel closest to or know best?
- Who on our family vine has taught you important lessons about life, and what are some of these lessons?
- Are there individuals on our family vine that we need to contact to tell them how much we love them?

Asking God

Say: Let us pray together as a family . . .

Let us share our prayers for the world—for our country and leaders, and for other countries and their leaders . . .

Let us share our prayers for the church, ministers, and other spiritual leaders . . .

Let us share our prayers for our friends, teachers, and others in our community . . .

Let us share our prayers for family members and our own specific needs . . .

Use the space provided below to make note of family prayer requests. Take a few minutes to review requests from the previous week.

Prayer Requests:

_____

_____

_____

_____

_____

Offering Ourselves to God

Pray aloud together:

God, we have read your Holy Word,
We have prayed together,
We have spent time with you,
We have experienced your love for us,
Now, we promise to love one another and others as you love us.
In the name of Christ. Amen.

Blessing One Another

Invite family members to bless one another. Some examples might be:

> "May God bless you, guide you, and be with you, today and always. In the name of Christ, Amen."

> "I love you, and I ask God to bless you."

> "God loves you just the way you are, and so do I!"

OUR HOME AS A PLACE FOR GOD

Jesus answered him, "Those who love me will keep my word, and my Father will love them, and we will come to them and make our home with them." —John 14:23

Supplies
- Bible(s)
- sacred candle, matches or lighter

Welcoming God

Gather as a family and light a candle as a symbolic way of inviting God to join you during this time together. Sit quietly for a moment so that everyone has the opportunity to relax his or her body, mind, and spirit.

Sharing With God

Say: If there is anything weighing on our minds and making it difficult to focus, let us share it now and then let it go.

Enter a quiet time when family members can share. You might go first and set the example by sharing anything that is weighing on your own mind.

Listening for God

Say: In this Scripture, Jesus tells us that he dwells with those who love him.

Read aloud John 14:23-29. Take turns reading the Scripture, or have a different family member read the Scripture passage each week.

Family Share and Reflection Time

Say: If we found out that God was actually coming to live in our home, what would we do to make our home ready? We would want it to be all nice and tidy and look like we were excited for God to come here. Let's act as if God is coming and clean our house!

Activity: Clean your house! Pick up toys, put clutter away, and get it in "company" shape. If cleaning up the house seems like too much work, or you get too much resistance from your children or teens, perhaps you could set the table or focus on making one room a place where guests would be welcome.

Discussion Questions:
- Did you enjoy cleaning up? What else would you rather have been doing?
- We cleaned up our house physically, but if God were really coming to live here, what kinds of spiritual things would we need to do more regularly?
- Do you think God lives in our home? In what ways does God live here?

- What does it mean to say that God makes a home within us?
- (For older children and teens) In what ways does our world need to be "cleaned up"? How would our world be different if everyone followed the example of Jesus? What can we do to live like Jesus more consistently—at home, at school, at work, and everywhere we go?

 Asking God

Say: Let us pray together as a family . . .

Let us share our prayers for the world—for our country and leaders, and for other countries and their leaders . . .

Let us share our prayers for the church, ministers, and other spiritual leaders . . .

Let us share our prayers for our friends, teachers, and others in our community . . .

Let us share our prayers for family members and our own specific needs . . .

Use the space provided below to make note of family prayer requests. Take a few minutes to review requests from the previous week.

Prayer Requests:

_____

_____

_____

_____

_____

Offering Ourselves to God

Pray aloud together:

God, we have read your Holy Word,
We have prayed together,
We have spent time with you,
We have experienced your love for us,
Now, we promise to love one another and others as you
    love us.
In the name of Christ. Amen.

Blessing One Another

Invite family members to bless one another. Some examples
might be:

"May God bless you, guide you, and be with you, today
    and always. In the name of Christ, Amen."

"I love you, and I ask God to bless you."

"God loves you just the way you are, and so do I!"

Praying for One Another

I am not asking [these things] on behalf of the world,
but on behalf of those whom you gave me, because they are yours.
—John 17:9

Supplies
- Bible(s)
- sacred candle, matches or lighter
- sheet of paper and pen or pencil for each family member
- crayons or markers for younger children

 ## Welcoming God

Gather as a family and light a candle as a symbolic way of inviting God to join you during this time together. Sit quietly for a moment so that everyone has the opportunity to relax his or her body, mind, and spirit.

Sharing With God

Say: If there is anything weighing on our minds and making it difficult to focus, let us share it now and then let it go.

Enter a quiet time when family members can share. You might go first and set the example by sharing anything that is weighing on your own mind.

Listening for God

Say: Jesus often spent time praying. In this Scripture, he is praying to God and asking God to watch over and take care of those he loves.

Read aloud John 17:1-11. Take turns reading the Scripture, or have a different family member read the Scripture passage each week.

 ## Family Share and Reflection Time

Say: We are going to spend time praying for those we love, just as Jesus did.

Activity: Have each family member write a prayer for the other members of the family. Gently remind them that it would be hurtful to pray for some members of the family and not for others. Small children can draw their prayers using pictures instead of words, or have an older sibling or parent write the words for them. After everyone has written or drawn a prayer, invite family members to take turns reading their prayers aloud or sharing their pictures.

Discussion Questions:
- Was it easy or awkward to read or share your prayer? Why?
- Do you pray for those you love regularly? Why or why not?
- If we were going to pray for you as a family, what would you ask us to pray about? What do you need? (Write down those requests mentioned and include them in your prayer time. See space provided on opposite page.)

 **Asking God**

Say: Let us pray together as a family . . .

Let us share our prayers for the world—for our country and leaders, and for other countries and their leaders . . .

Let us share our prayers for the church, ministers, and other spiritual leaders . . .

Let us share our prayers for our friends, teachers, and others in our community . . .

Let us share our prayers for family members and our own specific needs . . .

Use the space provided below to make note of any additional family prayer requests. Take a few minutes to review requests from the previous week.

Prayer Requests:

_____

_____

_____

_____

_____

Offering Ourselves to God

Pray aloud together:

God, we have read your Holy Word,
We have prayed together,
We have spent time with you,
We have experienced your love for us,

Now, we promise to love one another and others as you love us.

In the name of Christ. Amen.

Blessing One Another

Invite family members to bless one another. Some examples might be:

> "May God bless you, guide you, and be with you, today and always. In the name of Christ, Amen."

> "I love you, and I ask God to bless you."

> "God loves you just the way you are, and so do I!"

CELEBRATING THE BEGINNING OF THE CHURCH

When the day of Pentecost had come, they were all together in one place. And suddenly from heaven there came a sound like the rush of a violent wind, and it filled the entire house where they were sitting. —Acts 2:1-2

Supplies

- Bible(s)
- sacred candle, matches or lighter
- balloon for each family member

 ## Welcoming God

Gather as a family and light a candle as a symbolic way of inviting God to join you during this time together. Sit quietly for a moment so that everyone has the opportunity to relax his or her body, mind, and spirit.

Sharing With God

Say: If there is anything weighing on our minds and making it difficult to focus, let us share it now and then let it go.

Enter a quiet time when family members can share. You might go first and set the example by sharing anything that is weighing on your own mind.

Listening for God

Say: Pentecost is the day when the Christian church began. When Jesus died, his followers did not know what to do next, and they were afraid. On the day of Pentecost, the Spirit of God filled them, and they became brave and started the church of Jesus—the Christian church!

Read aloud Acts 2:1-21. Take turns reading the Scripture, or have a different family member read the Scripture passage each week.

 Family Share and Reflection Time

Say: We are going to use our balloons to remember and tell the story of Pentecost.

Activity: Retell the story of Pentecost. Begin by giving each family member a balloon. Tell them to shake their balloons without air as if they were people shaking, and remind your family of how scared Jesus' friends and followers were after he died. Then have them blow up their balloons, and remind them of how the Holy Spirit filled those scared people with courage and joy, inspiring them to preach to others. Then let go of the balloons at the same time as a celebration of the day! Do it several times, if you like!

Instead of telling the story to older children and teens, give each one a balloon and explain that being afraid is like being a limp balloon, and that this is how the disciples felt. Then explain that just as the Spirit of God gave the disciples courage, so the Spirit gives us courage. Have them blow up their balloons and let them go. Even teens like to watch balloons fly all over!

Discussion Questions:

- Why do you think Jesus' followers were so afraid after he died?
- What makes you afraid? Tell about a time when you were frightened.
- The Spirit of God filled the followers with courage. How does God help us when we are afraid? Share stories of times when God gave you courage.
- What can we do when we are afraid to remind ourselves that God is with us?

 ## Asking God

Say: Let us pray together as a family . . .

Let us share our prayers for the world—for our country and leaders, and for other countries and their leaders . . .
Let us share our prayers for the church, ministers, and other spiritual leaders . . .
Let us share our prayers for our friends, teachers, and others in our community . . .
Let us share our prayers for family members and our own specific needs . . .

Use the space provided below to make note of family prayer requests. Take a few minutes to review requests from the previous week.

Prayer Requests:

_____
_____
_____
_____
_____

Offering Ourselves to God

Pray aloud together:

God, we have read your Holy Word,
We have prayed together,
We have spent time with you,
We have experienced your love for us,
Now, we promise to love one another and others as you
    love us.
In the name of Christ. Amen.

Blessing One Another

Invite family members to bless one another. Some examples
might be:

"May God bless you, guide you, and be with you, today
    and always. In the name of Christ, Amen."

"I love you, and I ask God to bless you."

"God loves you just the way you are, and so do I!"

Heaven

*We rejoice in the hope
of the glory of God.*
—Romans 5:2b (NIV)

Supplies
- Bible(s)
- sacred candle, matches or lighter
- box of some kind

 ## Welcoming God

Gather as a family and light a candle as a symbolic way of inviting God to join you during this time together. Sit quietly for a moment so that everyone has the opportunity to relax his or her body, mind, and spirit.

Sharing With God

Say: If there is anything weighing on our minds and making it difficult to focus, let us share it now and then let it go.

Enter a quiet time when family members can share. You might go first and set the example by sharing anything that is weighing on your own mind.

Listening for God

Say: In this Scripture, Paul comforts us, saying that even though life can be hard sometimes, we can hope for good things to come, like living with Jesus in heaven.

Read aloud Romans 5:1-5. Take turns reading the Scripture, or have a different family member read the Scripture passage each week.

 Family Share and Reflection Time

Say: No one knows exactly what heaven is like. We know from the Bible that it is beautiful and that we won't need anything there because all our needs and wants will be supplied. Let's try and make "heaven in a box"!

Activity: Go on a journey around your home and look for things that are symbols of heaven for each of you. Perhaps someone's special blanket is a symbol of the comfort and security of heaven. Perhaps a piece of candy or a scented candle remind you of the beauty of heaven. As you collect the items, place them in the box. After everything is collected, sit in a circle around the box. Take out each item one at a time and pass it around so that you can experience the beauty of heaven.

Discussion Questions:
- What do you think heaven looks like?
- What do you think heaven feels like?
- What do you think heaven smells like?
- Who is in heaven now that you most would like to meet?

 **Asking God**

Say: Let us pray together as a family . . .

Let us share our prayers for the world—for our country and leaders, and for other countries and their leaders . . .
Let us share our prayers for the church, ministers, and other spiritual leaders . . .
Let us share our prayers for our friends, teachers, and others in our community . . .
Let us share our prayers for family members and our own specific needs . . .

Use the space provided below to make note of family prayer requests. Take a few minutes to review requests from the previous week.

Prayer Requests:

_____
_____
_____
_____
_____

Offering Ourselves to God

Pray aloud together:

God, we have read your Holy Word,
We have prayed together,
We have spent time with you,
We have experienced your love for us,

Now, we promise to love one another and others as you love us.
In the name of Christ. Amen.

Blessing One Another

Invite family members to bless one another. Some examples might be:

> "May God bless you, guide you, and be with you, today and always. In the name of Christ, Amen."

> "I love you, and I ask God to bless you."

> "God loves you just the way you are, and so do I!"

THE STORY OF NOAH'S ARK

God said to Noah, "I am going to put an end to all people, for the earth is filled with violence because of them. I am surely going to destroy both them and the earth. So make yourself an ark of cypress wood." —Genesis 6:13-14a (NIV)

Supplies
- Bible(s)
- sacred candle, matches or lighter

 ## Welcoming God

Gather as a family and light a candle as a symbolic way of inviting God to join you during this time together. Sit quietly for a moment so that everyone has the opportunity to relax his or her body, mind, and spirit.

Sharing With God

Say: If there is anything weighing on our minds and making it difficult to focus, let us share it now and then let it go.

Enter a quiet time when family members can share. You might go first and set the example by sharing anything that is weighing on your own mind.

Listening for God

Say: This is the story of Noah's Ark—a story about how God saved the world!

Read aloud Genesis 6:9-22. Take turns reading the Scripture, or have a different family member read the Scripture passage each week.

 # Family Share and Reflection Time

Say: Have you ever wondered how large Noah's ark really was? In Bible times, they did not use rulers. They used their bodies to measure. A cubit is measured from your longest finger to your elbow. The Bible says that Noah's ark was 300 cubits long and 50 cubits wide.

Activity: Measure your home to see if it is larger or smaller than Noah's ark using your forearms. Write down the size of your home and compare it to the size of the ark.

Discussion Questions:
- When the rains came, every animal and every person inside the ark was safe and secure. In what ways is our home like an ark?
- Do you feel safe and secure at home? Why or why not?
- What can we do as a family to make sure our home is a holy, safe place for all of us?

 **Asking God**

Say: Let us pray together as a family . . .

Let us share our prayers for the world—for our country and leaders, and for other countries and their leaders . . .

Let us share our prayers for the church, ministers, and other spiritual leaders . . .

Let us share our prayers for our friends, teachers, and others in our community . . .

Let us share our prayers for family members and our own specific needs . . .

Use the space provided below to make note of family prayer requests. Take a few minutes to review requests from the previous week.

Prayer Requests:

_____

_____

_____

_____

_____

Offering Ourselves to God

Pray aloud together:

God, we have read your Holy Word,
We have prayed together,
We have spent time with you,

We have experienced your love for us,
Now, we promise to love one another and others as you
   love us.
In the name of Christ. Amen.

Blessing One Another

Invite family members to bless one another. Some examples
might be:

> "May God bless you, guide you, and be with you, today
> and always. In the name of Christ, Amen."

> "I love you, and I ask God to bless you."

> "God loves you just the way you are, and so do I!"

BEING A BLESSING

The LORD had said to Abram, "Leave your country, your people and
your father's household and go to the land I will show you.
I will make you into a great nation and I will bless you; I will make
your name great, and you will be a blessing."
—Genesis 12:1-2 (NIV)

Supplies

- Bible(s)
- sacred candle, matches or lighter
- roll of aluminum foil (*optional for older children and teens:*
  tree branch or pipe cleaners, glue or tape)

 ## Welcoming God

Gather as a family and light a candle as a symbolic way of inviting God to join you during this time together. Sit quietly for a
moment so that everyone has the opportunity to relax his or her
body, mind, and spirit.

Sharing With God

Say: If there is anything weighing on our minds and making it
difficult to focus, let us share it now and then let it go.

Enter a quiet time when family members can share. You might go
first and set the example by sharing anything that is weighing on
your own mind.

Listening for God

Say: A long time ago, God called Abraham and Sarah to follow God. God promised that if they did as God asked, then God would bless them with as many descendents (children, grandchildren, great grandchildren, great-great grandchildren, and on and on) as there are stars in the sky. God kept God's promise, and we are the descendents of Abraham and Sarah. So was Jesus!

Read aloud Genesis 12:1-9. Take turns reading the Scripture, or have a different family member read the Scripture passage each week.

 ## Family Share and Reflection Time

Say: We are the children of Abraham and Sarah and King David and Jesus. We can be proud that we are from such a wonderful family!

Activity: Tear off pieces of the aluminum foil and work together to fold and create stars for all of the Bible characters you can remember. Then make stars representing your family—children, parents, grandparents, great grandparents, cousins, aunts, and uncles. Take a few minutes to look at how beautiful your family is—as beautiful as the stars that shine!

To make this activity a bit more creative for older children and teens, go outside and find a branch from a tree (or use pipe cleaners) and add the stars made from foil (attach with glue or tape). Use your creation as a centerpiece for the family table.

Another option for older children and teens is to go outside after dark (if it is a clear night) and gaze at the night sky. (If you are unable to do this, find a website on your computer that has images of the night sky.) Begin "counting" the stars by naming family members—immediate and then extended. When you can't think of any more family members, tell them to imagine that each star represents a distant family member. How does it feel to think that you are part of a family of that size? (Move on to the discussion questions, adapting them as necessary for the ages of your children.)

Discussion Questions:

- How does it feel to remember that we are all connected as family through Abraham, Sarah, and Jesus? How do you feel to be a relative of Bible characters?
- If we are all family, does that mean that our friends and neighbors are also our brothers and sisters?
- If we believe we are all family, how should we treat one another?

 Asking God

Say: Let us pray together as a family . . .

Let us share our prayers for the world—for our country and leaders, and for other countries and their leaders . . .

Let us share our prayers for the church, ministers, and other spiritual leaders . . .

Let us share our prayers for our friends, teachers, and others in our community . . .

Let us share our prayers for family members and our own specific needs . . .

Use the space provided below to make note of family prayer requests. Take a few minutes to review requests from the previous week.

Prayer Requests:

_____
_____
_____
_____
_____

Offering Ourselves to God

Pray aloud together:

> God, we have read your Holy Word,
> We have prayed together,
> We have spent time with you,
> We have experienced your love for us,
> Now, we promise to love one another and others as you
>   love us.
> In the name of Christ. Amen.

Blessing One Another

Invite family members to bless one another. Some examples might be:

> "May God bless you, guide you, and be with you, today
>   and always. In the name of Christ, Amen."

> "I love you, and I ask God to bless you."

> "God loves you just the way you are, and so do I!"

THE PARABLE OF THE MUSTARD SEED

"What shall we say the kingdom of God is like, or what parable shall we use to describe it? It is like a mustard seed, which is the smallest seed you plant in the ground. Yet when planted, it grows and becomes the largest of all garden plants."
—Mark 4:30-32a (NIV)

Supplies
- Bible(s)
- sacred candle, matches or lighter
- mustard seed

 ## Welcoming God

Gather as a family and light a candle as a symbolic way of inviting God to join you during this time together. Sit quietly for a moment so that everyone has the opportunity to relax his or her body, mind, and spirit.

Sharing With God

Say: If there is anything weighing on our minds and making it difficult to focus, let us share it now and then let it go.

Enter a quiet time when family members can share. You might go first and set the example by sharing anything that is weighing on your own mind.

Listening for God

Say: Jesus often used everyday things to explain what God's kingdom is like. In this Scripture, Jesus uses a very tiny mustard seed and explains that God can grow huge things out of the tiniest "seed." Great things can grow out of something as simple as a prayer or a kind action.

Read aloud Mark 4:26-34. Take turns reading the Scripture, or have a different family member read the Scripture passage each week.

 ## Family Share and Reflection Time

Say: This is a mustard seed. (Show the seed to your family.) See how very tiny it is! Jesus said that the tiniest thing can grow really huge! Let's demonstrate this by building something huge!

Activity: Place the mustard seed in the middle of the floor. Then have family members find things such as boxes, blocks, chairs, and pots and pans; and work together to build the tallest "mustard tree" you can! Have fun and be creative!

Challenge older children and teens to build a tall structure on their own using CDs, books, dominoes, or some other object they might choose. Encourage them to be creative and see how high they can make the structure without it falling. If you like, have a contest to see which family member can make the tallest "mustard tree."

Discussion Questions:

- Have you ever seen God "build" something in your life? Maybe an answered prayer or a miracle?
- Has someone ever done something small for you that made a huge difference to you? If so, tell about it.
- What small prayer do you have for God today? Do you think God will make something wonderful out of your prayer?

 ## Asking God

Say: Let us pray together as a family . . .

Let us share our prayers for the world—for our country and leaders, and for other countries and their leaders . . .

Let us share our prayers for the church, ministers, and other spiritual leaders . . .

Let us share our prayers for our friends, teachers, and others in our community . . .

Let us share our prayers for family members and our own specific needs . . .

Use the space provided below to make note of family prayer requests. Take a few minutes to review requests from the previous week.

Prayer Requests:

_____

_____

_____

_____

_____

Offering Ourselves to God

Pray aloud together:

God, we have read your Holy Word,
We have prayed together,
We have spent time with you,
We have experienced your love for us,
Now, we promise to love one another and others as you
    love us.
In the name of Christ. Amen.

Blessing One Another

Invite family members to bless one another. Some examples
might be:

"May God bless you, guide you, and be with you, today
    and always. In the name of Christ, Amen."

"I love you, and I ask God to bless you."

"God loves you just the way you are, and so do I!"

GIVING OUR SADNESS TO GOD

*As a deer longs for flowing streams, /
so my soul longs for you, O God.*
—*Psalm 42:1*

Supplies

- Bible(s)
- sacred candle, matches or lighter
- sheet of paper and crayons or markers for each family member

 ## Welcoming God

Gather as a family and light a candle as a symbolic way of inviting God to join you during this time together. Sit quietly for a moment so that everyone has the opportunity to relax his or her body, mind, and spirit.

Sharing With God

Say: If there is anything weighing on our minds and making it difficult to focus, let us share it now and then let it go.

Enter a quiet time when family members can share. You might go first and set the example by sharing anything that is weighing on your own mind.

Listening for God

Say: The Psalms are a collection of poems and songs written to express people's feelings to God. They are filled with images that express to God exactly how the writers felt. This psalm was written by someone who needed God very much!

Read aloud Psalm 42. Take turns reading the Scripture, or have a different family member read the Scripture passage each week.

 ## Family Share and Reflection Time

Say: There is an old way of listening to Scripture called *lectio divina* where the Scripture is read several times and people listen closely, trying to hear God. I am going to read this psalm several times, and then I want you to draw an image that came to your mind while you were listening to the words.

Activity: Invite your family to remain very quiet and listen as you read aloud Psalm 42 three times. Then ask each person to draw an image that came to mind as he or listened to the psalm. Share your drawings.

Discussion Questions:
- We all did not draw the same image. Why do you think we heard different things from the same Scripture?
- If you were writing a psalm, what would you want to share with God today? Are you happy? Scared? Lonely?
- Do you think there are any feelings we should not share with God? Why or why not?

 **Asking God**

Say: Let us pray together as a family . . .

Let us share our prayers for the world—for our country and leaders, and for other countries and their leaders . . .

Let us share our prayers for the church, ministers, and other spiritual leaders . . .

Let us share our prayers for our friends, teachers, and others in our community . . .

Let us share our prayers for family members and our own specific needs . . .

Use the space provided below to make note of family prayer requests. Take a few minutes to review requests from the previous week.

Prayer Requests:

_____
_____
_____
_____
_____

Offering Ourselves to God

Pray aloud together:

God, we have read your Holy Word,
We have prayed together,
We have spent time with you,
We have experienced your love for us,

Now, we promise to love one another and others as you
    love us.
In the name of Christ. Amen.

Blessing One Another

Invite family members to bless one another. Some examples
might be:

"May God bless you, guide you, and be with you, today
    and always. In the name of Christ, Amen."

"I love you, and I ask God to bless you."

"God loves you just the way you are, and so do I!"

ELIJAH AND ELISHA

*As they continued walking and talking, a chariot of fire
and horses of fire separated the two of them,
and Elijah ascended in a whirlwind into heaven.*
—*2 Kings 2:11*

Supplies

- Bible(s)
- sacred candle, matches or lighter
- paper cup
- crayons or markers or colored pencils

 ## Welcoming God

Gather as a family and light a candle as a symbolic way of inviting God to join you during this time together. Sit quietly for a moment so that everyone has the opportunity to relax his or her body, mind, and spirit.

Sharing With God

Say: If there is anything weighing on our minds and making it difficult to focus, let us share it now and then let it go.

Enter a quiet time when family members can share. You might go first and set the example by sharing anything that is weighing on your own mind.

Listening for God

Say: Elijah was a very famous prophet. It was predicted that he would return before the messiah came. Jewish people have a special ritual each year called a Seder meal. They set a place at their Seder meal table in hopes that Elijah will arrive and celebrate the Seder with them. Let us hear a little bit of the story of Elijah.

Read: 2 Kings 2:1-2, 6-14. Take turns reading the Scripture, or have a different family member read the Scripture passage each week.

 Family Share and Reflection Time

Say: We no longer wait for Elijah to come because we have Jesus, our messiah, with us all the time! Tonight, let's take the Seder tradition, change it a bit, and make a cup in honor of Jesus.

Activity: Take a paper cup and have each member of the family draw on it symbols of Jesus and his love. They might be scenes from his life or symbols he used as he taught, such as a mustard seed or grapevine. After the cup is decorated with symbols, fill it with water and place it on your dinner table to remind you that Jesus, who is our Living Water, has come and is with us whenever we gather. At your next family meal, set an extra place at the table for Jesus, putting the special cup at this place. Give thanks once again that Jesus is present with you!

Discussion Questions:

- Why is a cup a good symbol of Jesus?
- What do you think Jesus meant when he said he was "living water" (see John 4)?
- How does it make you feel to know that Jesus is here with us?
- What other things can we give thanks for and celebrate together?

 Asking God

Say: Let us pray together as a family . . .

Let us share our prayers for the world—for our country and leaders, and for other countries and their leaders . . .

Let us share our prayers for the church, ministers, and other spiritual leaders . . .

Let us share our prayers for our friends, teachers, and others in our community . . .

Let us share our prayers for family members and our own specific needs . . .

Use the space provided below to make note of family prayer requests. Take a few minutes to review requests from the previous week.

Prayer Requests:

_____
_____
_____
_____
_____

Offering Ourselves to God

Pray aloud together:

> God, we have read your Holy Word,
> We have prayed together,
> We have spent time with you,
> We have experienced your love for us,
> Now, we promise to love one another and others as you
> love us.
> In the name of Christ. Amen.

Blessing One Another

Invite family members to bless one another. Some examples might be:

> "May God bless you, guide you, and be with you, today
> and always. In the name of Christ, Amen."

> "I love you, and I ask God to bless you."

> "God loves you just the way you are, and so do I!"

JESUS AS A HELPER

"Come to me, all you that are weary and are carrying heavy burdens, and I will give you rest. Take my yoke upon you, and learn from me; for I am gentle and humble in heart, and you will find rest for your souls." —Matthew 11:28-29

Supplies
- Bible(s)
- sacred candle, matches or lighter
- item in your house that one person could not lift alone but that you could lift together (e.g., chair or small couch)

 ## Welcoming God

Gather as a family and light a candle as a symbolic way of inviting God to join you during this time together. Sit quietly for a moment so that everyone has the opportunity to relax his or her body, mind, and spirit.

Sharing With God

Say: If there is anything weighing on our minds and making it difficult to focus, let us share it now and then let it go.

Enter a quiet time when family members can share. You might go first and set the example by sharing anything that is weighing on your own mind.

Listening for God

Say: This is a very well known Scripture passage in which Jesus tells us that he will help carry our burdens and worries.

Read aloud Matthew 11:25-30. Take turns reading the Scripture, or have a different family member read the Scripture passage each week.

 Family Share and Reflection Time

Say: We all have burdens we carry. Maybe we have hurt feelings, are worried about something, or are scared of failing a certain class in school. This Scripture tells us that we never have to carry those burdens alone. Jesus is always with us. This activity will help us remember that things are always heavier and more difficult when we face them alone.

Activity: Have each member of the family try to lift the heavy object by himself or herself (not push or scoot it, but lift it). Then, as a family, lift it together. You might try lifting several things around your house.

Discussion Questions:
- What burdens are you carrying?
- How can we, as a family, help you carry them as we just did in our activity? What can we do to help make your burdens lighter?
- How can praying help us when our burdens are heavy? How does Jesus help to carry our burdens?

 **Asking God**

Say: Let us pray together as a family . . .

>Let us share our prayers for the world—for our country and leaders, and for other countries and their leaders . . .
>
>Let us share our prayers for the church, ministers, and other spiritual leaders . . .
>
>Let us share our prayers for our friends, teachers, and others in our community . . .
>
>Let us share our prayers for family members and our own specific needs . . .

Use the space provided below to make note of family prayer requests. Take a few minutes to review requests from the previous week.

Prayer Requests:

_____

_____

_____

_____

_____

Offering Ourselves to God

Pray aloud together:

>God, we have read your Holy Word,
>We have prayed together,
>We have spent time with you,
>We have experienced your love for us,

Now, we promise to love one another and others as you love us.
In the name of Christ. Amen.

Blessing One Another

Invite family members to bless one another. Some examples might be:

"May God bless you, guide you, and be with you, today and always. In the name of Christ, Amen."

"I love you, and I ask God to bless you."

"God loves you just the way you are, and so do I!"

THE SHEMA: A SACRED PRAYER

"You shall love the Lord your God with all your heart,
and with all your soul, and with all your strength,
and with all your mind; and your neighbor as yourself."
—Luke 10:27

Supplies
- Bible(s)
- sacred candle, matches or lighter

 ## Welcoming God

Gather as a family and light a candle as a symbolic way of inviting God to join you during this time together. Sit quietly for a moment so that everyone has the opportunity to relax his or her body, mind, and spirit.

Sharing With God

Say: If there is anything weighing on our minds and making it difficult to focus, let us share it now and then let it go.

Enter a quiet time when family members can share. You might go first and set the example by sharing anything that is weighing on your own mind.

Listening for God

Say: In this passage Jesus recites Scripture he learned as a child. It is called the Shema, and it is found in Deuteronomy 6:4-5. Moses first recited this prayer to God's people, asking them to say it several times a day and to post it on the doorframes of their houses. Children recited the Shema as a bedtime prayer. In this story, Jesus reminds us of the beauty and truth of this prayer, adding the instruction to love our neighbors as ourselves.

Read aloud Luke 10:25-28. Take turns reading the Scripture, or have a different family member read the Scripture passage each week.

 # Family Share and Reflection Time

Say: As a Jew, Jesus would have hung the words of the Shema on the door to his house, and each time he left or entered his home he would have been reminded to love God with all his heart, soul, and might. When asked what the greatest commandment was, Jesus teaches the Shema and adds a second command: to love our neighbors as ourselves. In this activity, we will bless all the doorways in our home. Then, each time we walk through a door in our home, we will try to remember to love God and others.

Activity: Stand in each doorway of your home together and have one person read Luke 10:27. Then, as a family, say, "Help us to be a loving family, O God." Let a different family member recite the verse each time. Don't forget to bless all the doorways in your home, including bathrooms! By the time you are finished, you probably will have memorized the Scripture.

Discussion Questions:
- Our doorways will now remind us to love God. Are there other parts of our house that might remind us about God?
- What are some ways we can be more loving inside our home?
- What are some ways we can be more loving outside our home?
- Do you think other doorways might remind us to love God and others, such as doorways at school or work or church?

 Asking God

Say: Let us pray together as a family . . .

Let us share our prayers for the world—for our country and leaders, and for other countries and their leaders . . .
Let us share our prayers for the church, ministers, and other spiritual leaders . . .
Let us share our prayers for our friends, teachers, and others in our community . . .
Let us share our prayers for family members and our own specific needs . . .

Use the space provided on the next page to make note of family prayer requests. Take a few minutes to review requests from the previous week.

Prayer Requests:

_____

_____

_____

_____

_____

Offering Ourselves to God

Pray aloud together:

> God, we have read your Holy Word,
> We have prayed together,
> We have spent time with you,
> We have experienced your love for us,
> Now, we promise to love one another and others as you
> love us.
> In the name of Christ. Amen.

Blessing One Another

Invite family members to bless one another. Some examples might be:

> "May God bless you, guide you, and be with you, today and always. In the name of Christ, Amen."

> "I love you, and I ask God to bless you."

> "God loves you just the way you are, and so do I!"

MARY AND MARTHA

The Lord answered her, "Martha, Martha, you are worried and distracted by many things; there is need of only one thing. Mary has chosen the better part, which will not be taken away from her."
—Luke 10:41-42

Supplies
- Bible(s)
- sacred candle, matches or lighter
- sheet(s) of paper
- pen(s) and highlighter(s)

Welcoming God

Gather as a family and light a candle as a symbolic way of inviting God to join you during this time together. Sit quietly for a moment so that everyone has the opportunity to relax his or her body, mind, and spirit.

Sharing With God

Say: If there is anything weighing on our minds and making it difficult to focus, let us share it now and then let it go.

Enter a quiet time when family members can share. You might go first and set the example by sharing anything that is weighing on your own mind.

Listening for God

Say: Mary and Martha were very good friends with Jesus. Once, when he was visiting them, Martha was cooking dinner and working hard while her sister was sitting and listening to Jesus. Let's hear the story.

Read aloud Luke 10:38-42. Take turns reading the Scripture, or have a different family member read the Scripture passage each week.

 ## Family Share and Reflection Time

Say: In this story, Martha was working very hard and had no time to sit and listen to Jesus. Mary had things to do as well, but she decided that it was more important to listen to Jesus than to get everything done around the house. Jesus told Martha that sometimes she needed to stop "doing" things and make more time for him. We are going to make a list of all the things we do each day and then see if there are any things we need to change to make more time for Jesus.

Activity: Make a time chart of a normal day for your family. Include travel time in the car, meal preparation time, and television and game time. Allow older children and teens to create time charts of their own "typical day"—or week if activities vary significantly from day to day. Using the marker(s), highlight times where perhaps more time for Jesus could be made.

Discussion Questions:
- Mary was able to sit and listen to Jesus. How do we spend time with Jesus?
- Would you like to try to spend more time with Jesus? If so, what changes can you make to create more time with him?
- In what ways can we, as a family, create more opportunities for us to spend time with Jesus?

 ## Asking God

Say: Let us pray together as a family . . .

Let us share our prayers for the world—for our country and leaders, and for other countries and their leaders . . .

Let us share our prayers for the church, ministers, and other spiritual leaders . . .

Let us share our prayers for our friends, teachers, and others in our community . . .

Let us share our prayers for family members and our own specific needs . . .

Use the space provided below to make note of family prayer requests. Take a few minutes to review requests from the previous week.

Prayer Requests:

_____

_____

_____

_____

_____

Offering Ourselves to God

Pray aloud together:

> God, we have read your Holy Word,
> We have prayed together,
> We have spent time with you,
> We have experienced your love for us,
> Now, we promise to love one another and others as you
>   love us.
> In the name of Christ. Amen.

Blessing One Another

Invite family members to bless one another. Some examples
might be:

> "May God bless you, guide you, and be with you, today
>   and always. In the name of Christ, Amen."

> "I love you, and I ask God to bless you."

> "God loves you just the way you are, and so do I!"

ASKING GOD FOR THE THINGS WE NEED

"If you then, who are evil, know how to give good gifts to your children, how much more will the heavenly Father give the Holy Spirit to those who ask him!" —Luke 11:13

Supplies
- Bible(s)
- sacred candle, matches or lighter
- three lunch bags with a different "good thing" inside (Examples: flower, snack, kind note)

 ## Welcoming God

Gather as a family and light a candle as a symbolic way of inviting God to join you during this time together. Sit quietly for a moment so that everyone has the opportunity to relax his or her body, mind, and spirit.

Sharing With God

Say: If there is anything weighing on our minds and making it difficult to focus, let us share it now and then let it go.

Enter a quiet time when family members can share. You might go first and set the example by sharing anything that is weighing on your own mind.

Listening for God

Say: In this passage, the followers of Jesus asked him to tell them about prayer. This is what Jesus taught them.

Read aloud Luke 11:1-13. Take turns reading the Scripture, or have a different family member read the Scripture passage each week.

 ## Family Share and Reflection Time

Say: Jesus taught his followers that when we ask God for anything, we can expect God to give us good things. God would never hurt us or give us something terrible because we asked. This game will remind us that we can expect good things from God.

Activity: In advance, put one "good thing" inside each lunch sack. Hold up one bag at a time and let your family members try to guess what is inside. If you want, let older children and teens take turns hiding a "good thing" in each bag and having the rest of the family guess what is inside. Enjoy playing this game together. Each time you open a bag and see what is inside, remind everyone that just like the good things in the bags, God gives us good things when we ask.

Discussion Questions:
- Do you think we can ask God for anything, or do you think there are things we should not ask for? Why?

- Do you think God ever gets angry with us for asking? Why or why not?
- When have you asked God for something in a prayer? What do you need to ask for today?

 Asking God

Say: Let us pray together as a family . . .

Let us share our prayers for the world—for our country and leaders, and for other countries and their leaders . . .

Let us share our prayers for the church, ministers, and other spiritual leaders . . .

Let us share our prayers for our friends, teachers, and others in our community . . .

Let us share our prayers for family members and our own specific needs . . .

Use the space provided below to make note of family prayer requests. Take a few minutes to review requests from the previous week.

Prayer Requests:

_____

_____

_____

_____

_____

Offering Ourselves to God

Pray aloud together:

God, we have read your Holy Word,
We have prayed together,
We have spent time with you,
We have experienced your love for us,
Now, we promise to love one another and others as you
love us.
In the name of Christ. Amen.

Blessing One Another

Invite family members to bless one another. Some examples
might be:

"May God bless you, guide you, and be with you, today
and always. In the name of Christ, Amen."

"I love you, and I ask God to bless you."

"God loves you just the way you are, and so do I!"

FEEDING THE FIVE THOUSAND

*Taking the five loaves and the two fish, he looked up to heaven, and
blessed and broke the loaves, and gave them to the disciples, and
the disciples gave them to the crowds. And all ate and were filled.*
—Matthew 14:19-20a

Supplies

- Bible(s)
- sacred candle, matches or lighter
- two bags of un-popped microwave popcorn

 ## Welcoming God

Gather as a family and light a candle as a symbolic way of inviting God to join you during this time together. Sit quietly for a
moment so that everyone has the opportunity to relax his or her
body, mind, and spirit.

Sharing With God

Say: If there is anything weighing on our minds and making it
difficult to focus, let us share it now and then let it go.

Enter a quiet time when family members can share. You might go
first and set the example by sharing anything that is weighing on
your own mind.

Listening for God

Say: This is a wonderful story of a time when Jesus fed 5,000 people with only five loaves of bread and two fish.

Read aloud Matthew 14:13-21. Take turns reading the Scripture, or have a different family member read the Scripture passage each week.

 ## Family Share and Reflection Time

Say: Jesus took five loaves of bread and two fish and was able to feed 5,000 people. This story reminds us that because Jesus is with us, we will always have enough.

Activity: Open one of the bags of popcorn and see how small the popcorn looks. Then pop the other bag and watch it grow larger as it pops. Enjoy the popcorn and while you do, share times when you did not think you had enough of something—talents, skills, money, and so forth—yet God supplied your needs.

Discussion Questions:
- Is there anything you need God to help you have more of—such as money for things you need, intelligence for doing well at school, or talents for sports or music? What is it?
- The uncooked popcorn did not look like enough to feed all of us. The five loaves and two fish did not look like enough to feed 5,000 people, but they were. Do you think maybe

you already have enough of what you need? How might this be true?

- What can we do to support you in your times of doubt?

 Asking God

Say: Let us pray together as a family . . .

Let us share our prayers for the world—for our country and leaders, and for other countries and their leaders . . .

Let us share our prayers for the church, ministers, and other spiritual leaders . . .

Let us share our prayers for our friends, teachers, and others in our community . . .

Let us share our prayers for family members and our own specific needs . . .

Use the space provided below to make note of family prayer requests. Take a few minutes to review requests from the previous week.

Prayer Requests:

_____

_____

_____

_____

_____

Offering Ourselves to God

Pray aloud together:

> God, we have read your Holy Word,
> We have prayed together,
> We have spent time with you,
> We have experienced your love for us,
> Now, we promise to love one another and others as you
> love us.
> In the name of Christ. Amen.

Blessing One Another

Invite family members to bless one another. Some examples might be:

> "May God bless you, guide you, and be with you, today
> and always. In the name of Christ, Amen."

> "I love you, and I ask God to bless you."

> "God loves you just the way you are, and so do I!"

SINGING TO GOD

O give thanks to the LORD, call on his name, /
make known his deeds among the peoples. /
Sing to him, sing praises to him; /
tell of all his wonderful works.
—Psalm 105:1-2

Supplies
- Bible(s)
- sacred candle, matches or lighter
- paper and pencil or pen

 ## Welcoming God

Gather as a family and light a candle as a symbolic way of inviting God to join you during this time together. Sit quietly for a moment so that everyone has the opportunity to relax his or her body, mind, and spirit.

Sharing With God

Say: If there is anything weighing on our minds and making it difficult to focus, let us share it now and then let it go.

Enter a quiet time when family members can share. You might go first and set the example by sharing anything that is weighing on your own mind.

Listening for God

Say: Psalm 105 reminds us that God is wonderful and we should sing God's praises! In fact, in Old and New Testament days, psalms were sung as songs of praise!

Read aloud Psalm 105. Take turns reading the Scripture, or have a different family member read the Scripture passage each week.

 Family Share and Reflection Time

Say: This psalm is a song telling about some of the wonderful things God did for God's people. God does wonderful things for us! Let's write a song and sing about God!

Activity: Begin by making a list of the wonderful things about God, such as, "God is loving," "God answers our prayers," "God gave Dad/Mom a new job," or "God healed Granny's illness." Then, using a familiar tune such as "Twinkle, Twinkle, Little Star" or "Mary Had a Little Lamb," write a song of praise together and sing it! Older children and teens may enjoy writing a song of praise to one of their favorite tunes and teaching it to you.

Discussion Questions:
- If you were to write a song about God, what story from your own journey with God would you write about? Would it be a happy or sad psalm?
- What is your favorite song or hymn and why? Does it remind you of God; and if so, how?

 **Asking God**

Say: Let us pray together as a family . . .

Let us share our prayers for the world—for our country and leaders, and for other countries and their leaders . . .

Let us share our prayers for the church, ministers, and other spiritual leaders . . .

Let us share our prayers for our friends, teachers, and others in our community . . .

Let us share our prayers for family members and our own specific needs . . .

Use the space provided below to make note of family prayer requests. Take a few minutes to review requests from the previous week.

Prayer Requests:

_____

_____

_____

_____

_____

Offering Ourselves to God

Pray aloud together:

God, we have read your Holy Word,
We have prayed together,
We have spent time with you,

We have experienced your love for us,
Now, we promise to love one another and others as you
love us.
In the name of Christ. Amen.

Blessing One Another

Invite family members to bless one another. Some examples
might be:

"May God bless you, guide you, and be with you, today
and always. In the name of Christ, Amen."

"I love you, and I ask God to bless you."

"God loves you just the way you are, and so do I!"

MAKING GOOD GRAPE JUICE FOR GOD

My beloved had a vineyard / on a very fertile hill. /
He dug it and cleared it of stones, / and planted it with choice vines;
/ he built a watchtower in the midst of it, /
and hewed out a wine vat in it; / he expected it to yield grapes, /
but it yielded wild grapes. —Isaiah 5:1b-2

Supplies
- Bible(s)
- sacred candle, matches or lighter
- cup for every family member
- two pitchers of juice—one that is sweet, such as grape juice or lemonade, and one that is sour, such as lemon juice diluted with water

 ## Welcoming God

Gather as a family and light a candle as a symbolic way of inviting God to join you during this time together. Sit quietly for a moment so that everyone has the opportunity to relax his or her body, mind, and spirit.

Sharing With God

Say: If there is anything weighing on our minds and making it difficult to focus, let us share it now and then let it go.

Enter a quiet time when family members can share. You might go first and set the example by sharing anything that is weighing on your own mind.

Listening for God

Say: Many times in Scripture, the people of God are compared to grapes. Sometimes they listen to and follow God and are compared to good grape juice, and other times they refuse to follow God and are compared to sour grape juice. This is a story about God building a vineyard and being disappointed with the juice!

Read aloud Isaiah 5:1-4. Take turns reading the Scripture, or have a different family member read the Scripture passage each week.

Family Share and Reflection Time

Say: In this story from the Book of Isaiah, God worked very hard to make a vineyard. When God was finished and tasted the juice, it was sour. The vineyard represents the world God made, and the grapes represent the people who disappointed God by not appreciating God's world. This time together will help us understand how God felt.

Activity: Do some kind of exercise until you all are very hot and thirsty. Run around the outside of your house or play an outdoor game together. Older children and teens might enjoy taking you on in a game of basketball, kickball, softball, soccer, or tennis. If it is cold or raining outside, find a safe indoor activity that will get your heart pumping, such as doing sit-ups or jumping jacks, dancing, or playing an interactive video game (like Nintendo Wii) if you have one. Explain that this might be how God felt after making the vineyard, because God had worked very hard. Give everyone a taste of the sour juice and discuss how disappointing it is to taste sour juice after working so hard. Then enjoy the sweet juice!

Discussion Questions:

- In this story, God is the one who built the vineyard. What good things has God built for us and given us?
- After God built the vineyard, the grapes were sour. What actions of ours are like sour grapes to God?
- What actions do we do that are like sweet grape juice to God?
- Do we more often act like sour juice or sweet juice toward one another? Share examples of each.

 Asking God

Say: Let us pray together as a family . . .

Let us share our prayers for the world—for our country and leaders, and for other countries and their leaders . . .

Let us share our prayers for the church, ministers, and other spiritual leaders . . .

Let us share our prayers for our friends, teachers, and others in our community . . .

Let us share our prayers for family members and our own specific needs . . .

Use the space provided below to make note of family prayer requests. Take a few minutes to review requests from the previous week.

Prayer Requests:

_____

_____

_____

_____

_____

Offering Ourselves to God

Pray aloud together:

> God, we have read your Holy Word,
> We have prayed together,
> We have spent time with you,
> We have experienced your love for us,
> Now, we promise to love one another and others as you
> love us.
> In the name of Christ. Amen.

Blessing One Another

Invite family members to bless one another. Some examples might be:

> "May God bless you, guide you, and be with you, today
> and always. In the name of Christ, Amen."

> "I love you, and I ask God to bless you."

> "God loves you just the way you are, and so do I!"

PETER, THE ROCK

"And I tell you, you are Peter, and on this rock I will build my church, and the gates of Hades will not prevail against it."
—Matthew 16:18

Supplies
- Bible(s)
- sacred candle, matches or lighter
- nametag and pen for each family member (use pre-made nametags or make your own)

 ## Welcoming God

Gather as a family and light a candle as a symbolic way of inviting God to join you during this time together. Sit quietly for a moment so that everyone has the opportunity to relax his or her body, mind, and spirit.

Sharing With God

Say: If there is anything weighing on our minds and making it difficult to focus, let us share it now and then let it go.

Enter a quiet time when family members can share. You might go first and set the example by sharing anything that is weighing on your own mind.

Listening for God

Say: Simon was one of Jesus' disciples. Jesus asked a difficult question and Simon answered correctly. Jesus saw that Simon was very special and renamed him Peter, which means "rock." Jesus told him that he would be a leader in the church after Jesus died. Jesus' words were true! Let us read this story.

Read aloud Matthew 16:13-20. Take turns reading the Scripture, or have a different family member read the Scripture passage each week.

 ## Family Share and Reflection Time

Say: Jesus renamed Simon as Peter, which means "rock," because Jesus was going to make Peter strong and brave so that he might be an important leader in the church. In this activity, we are going to share the things we admire about each other.

Activity: Have each person write his or her name on a nametag and then pass it to each family member so that everyone may write a word or characteristic he or she admires about that person. Younger children might want to draw a symbol instead of writing a word. When you are done, have each person read all of the words or characteristics on his or her nametag and then put it on.

Discussion Questions:
- How did it feel to hear how special the other members of the family think you are?

- If you were to describe yourself, would any of the descriptions on your nametag be things you would list? Why or why not?
- What name do you think Jesus would rename you if he were here right now and why?

 Asking God

Say: Let us pray together as a family . . .

Let us share our prayers for the world—for our country and leaders, and for other countries and their leaders . . .

Let us share our prayers for the church, ministers, and other spiritual leaders . . .

Let us share our prayers for our friends, teachers, and others in our community . . .

Let us share our prayers for family members and our own specific needs . . .

Use the space provided below to make note of family prayer requests. Take a few minutes to review requests from the previous week.

Prayer Requests:

_____

_____

_____

_____

_____

Offering Ourselves to God

Pray aloud together:

> God, we have read your Holy Word,
> We have prayed together,
> We have spent time with you,
> We have experienced your love for us,
> Now, we promise to love one another and others as you
> love us.
> In the name of Christ. Amen.

Blessing One Another

Invite family members to bless one another. Some examples might be:

> "May God bless you, guide you, and be with you, today and always. In the name of Christ, Amen."

> "I love you, and I ask God to bless you."

> "God loves you just the way you are, and so do I!"

BEING LOVING

Let love be genuine; hate what is evil, hold fast to what is good; love one another with mutual affection . . . —Romans 12:9-10a

Supplies

- Bible(s)
- sacred candle, matches or lighter
- sheet of paper cut into strips—one for each family member
- pencil or pen for each family member
- roll of tape

 ## Welcoming God

Gather as a family and light a candle as a symbolic way of inviting God to join you during this time together. Sit quietly for a moment so that everyone has the opportunity to relax his or her body, mind, and spirit.

Sharing With God

Say: If there is anything weighing on our minds and making it difficult to focus, let us share it now and then let it go.

Enter a quiet time when family members can share. You might go first and set the example by sharing anything that is weighing on your own mind.

Listening for God

Say: Paul was an early follower of Jesus who taught many people about the love of Jesus. In this Scripture, Paul writes a beautiful description of love and how we should love one another, as Jesus has loved us.

Read aloud Romans 12:9-21. Take turns reading the Scripture, or have a different family member read the Scripture passage each week.

 # Family Share and Reflection Time

Say: Paul wrote beautiful things about love. We are going to write about love as well and work together to create a description of love. As we write, let's think about God's love for us, the ways Jesus taught us to love, and the ways we should treat others we love.

Activity: Give each family member a strip of paper and a pen. Have them sit quietly and think about God's love for us and the love we have for others. Then have each person write one sentence about love. Have younger children dictate their sentences to you. Read the sentences aloud and decide together what order to put them in. Tape the sentences together and read the entire poem you have created.

Discussion Questions:

- Paul wrote to people who had never heard of God's love. Do you think there are still people in the world who have not heard of God or God's love expressed to us through Jesus?

- How can we reach out to people in the world who have never heard of God or Jesus?
- Do you know anyone who does not believe in God or Jesus? If so, how can you show God's love to this person? What might you say and/or do?
- How can we reach out as a family to those who do not know the love of God/Jesus?

 Asking God

Say: Let us pray together as a family . . .

Let us share our prayers for the world—for our country and leaders, and for other countries and their leaders . . .

Let us share our prayers for the church, ministers, and other spiritual leaders . . .

Let us share our prayers for our friends, teachers, and others in our community . . .

Let us share our prayers for family members and our own specific needs . . .

Use the space provided below to make note of family prayer requests. Take a few minutes to review requests from the previous week.

Prayer Requests:

_____

_____

_____

_____

_____

Offering Ourselves to God

Pray aloud together:

> God, we have read your Holy Word,
> We have prayed together,
> We have spent time with you,
> We have experienced your love for us,
> Now, we promise to love one another and others as you
>   love us.
> In the name of Christ. Amen.

Blessing One Another

Invite family members to bless one another. Some examples might be:

> "May God bless you, guide you, and be with you, today
>   and always. In the name of Christ, Amen."

> "I love you, and I ask God to bless you."

> "God loves you just the way you are, and so do I!"

WHERE TWO GATHER,
THERE I AM

"Truly I tell you, if two of you agree on earth about anything you ask, it will be done for you by my Father in heaven. For where two or three are gathered in my name, I am there among them."
—Matthew 18:19-20

Supplies
- Bible(s)
- sacred candle, matches or lighter

 ## Welcoming God

Gather as a family and light a candle as a symbolic way of inviting God to join you during this time together. Sit quietly for a moment so that everyone has the opportunity to relax his or her body, mind, and spirit.

Sharing With God

Say: If there is anything weighing on our minds and making it difficult to focus, let us share it now and then let it go.

Enter a quiet time when family members can share. You might go first and set the example by sharing anything that is weighing on your own mind.

Listening for God

Say: In this Scripture, Jesus reminds us that we need one another all the time—to help each other solve problems, to pray for each other, and to worship together.

Read aloud Matthew 18:15-20. Take turns reading the Scripture, or have a different family member read the Scripture passage each week.

 ## Family Share and Reflection Time

Say: In this Scripture Jesus reminds us that we need each other all the time. We were not made to be alone, and that is why we are a family—to support and help one another. In this time together, we are going to join together in prayer. Jesus told us that whenever we gather, he will be with us and will answer our prayers.

Activity: Form a prayer circle. (Sit in a circle and hold hands.) Have each family member share a prayer request, pausing for a time after each request so that family members may pray silently or, if they are comfortable, aloud.

Do not rush this prayer exercise. Enjoy being together and feeling God's presence as you gather and pray.

Discussion Questions:
- Do you prefer praying alone or praying with others? Why? How are the two prayer experiences alike and different?

- Do you think we need to spend time praying in both ways? Why or why not?
- How did it feel to be prayed for by your family members? Was it comfortable or uncomfortable? What could have made it more comfortable for you?

 ## Asking God

Say: Let us pray together as a family . . .

Let us share our prayers for the world—for our country and leaders, and for other countries and their leaders . . .

Let us share our prayers for the church, ministers, and other spiritual leaders . . .

Let us share our prayers for our friends, teachers, and others in our community . . .

Let us share our prayers for family members and our own specific needs . . .

Use the space provided below to make note of family prayer requests (you may wish to write down those mentioned during the prayer circle activity). Take a few minutes to review requests from the previous week.

Prayer Requests:

_____

_____

_____

_____

_____

Offering Ourselves to God

Pray aloud together:

> God, we have read your Holy Word,
> We have prayed together,
> We have spent time with you,
> We have experienced your love for us,
> Now, we promise to love one another and others as you
> love us.
> In the name of Christ. Amen.

Blessing One Another

Invite family members to bless one another. Some examples might be:

> "May God bless you, guide you, and be with you, today
> and always. In the name of Christ, Amen."

> "I love you, and I ask God to bless you."

> "God loves you just the way you are, and so do I!"

FORGIVENESS

*Peter came and said to him, "Lord, if another member
of the church sins against me, how often should I forgive?
As many as seven times?" Jesus said to him, "Not seven times, but,
I tell you, seventy-seven times." —Matthew 18:21-22*

Supplies
- Bible(s)
- sacred candle, matches or lighter
- large bag of uncooked beans
- large bowl

 ## Welcoming God

Gather as a family and light a candle as a symbolic way of inviting God to join you during this time together. Sit quietly for a moment so that everyone has the opportunity to relax his or her body, mind, and spirit.

Sharing With God

Say: If there is anything weighing on our minds and making it difficult to focus, let us share it now and then let it go.

Enter a quiet time when family members can share. You might go first and set the example by sharing anything that is weighing on your own mind.

Listening for God

Say: We all get hurt sometimes by the things others say and do. So did Jesus and his disciples. One day Peter asked Jesus how many times we should forgive someone. Let's listen to what Jesus told him.

Read aloud Matthew 18:21-35. Take turns reading the Scripture, or have a different family member read the Scripture passage each week.

 ## Family Share and Reflection Time

Say: We're going to do something to show us just how many times Jesus said we are to forgive.

Activity: Place seven beans in a bowl and talk about how forgiving someone seven times is a lot. Then count out seventy beans seven times to discover just how forgiving Jesus expects us to be!

For older children and teens, you might want to have them do push-ups instead of count beans. First have them do seven push-ups, and talk about how difficult forgiving seven times might be. Then have them try to do seventy push-ups. After they get very tired, discuss how difficult it can be to forgive seventy times. Forgiveness is hard work!

Discussion Questions:
- Were you surprised by how many beans seven times seventy is? What does that tell you about how forgiving Jesus asks us to be?

- Is there anyone in your life who needs your forgiveness over and over? (Instruct family members not to say names out loud.)
- Is it difficult or easy to forgive someone over and over? Why?
- Do you think God forgives us over and over? How many times? How does this make you feel?

 ## Asking God

Say: Let us pray together as a family . . .

Let us share our prayers for the world—for our country and leaders, and for other countries and their leaders . . .

Let us share our prayers for the church, ministers, and other spiritual leaders . . .

Let us share our prayers for our friends, teachers, and others in our community . . .

Let us share our prayers for family members and our own specific needs . . .

Use the space provided below to make note of family prayer requests. Take a few minutes to review requests from the previous week.

Prayer Requests:

_____

_____

_____

_____

_____

Offering Ourselves to God

Pray aloud together:

> God, we have read your Holy Word,
> We have prayed together,
> We have spent time with you,
> We have experienced your love for us,
> Now, we promise to love one another and others as you
> love us.
> In the name of Christ. Amen.

Blessing One Another

Invite family members to bless one another. Some examples might be:

> "May God bless you, guide you, and be with you, today and always. In the name of Christ, Amen."

> "I love you, and I ask God to bless you."

> "God loves you just the way you are, and so do I!"

PRAYING FOR THOSE WHO LEAD US

I urge that supplications, prayers, intercessions, and thanksgivings be made for everyone, for kings and all who are in high positions . . .
—*1 Timothy 2:1-2a*

Supplies
- Bible(s)
- sacred candle, matches or lighter
- sheet of paper
- pen or pencil

 ## Welcoming God

Gather as a family and light a candle as a symbolic way of inviting God to join you during this time together. Sit quietly for a moment so that everyone has the opportunity to relax his or her body, mind, and spirit.

Sharing With God

Say: If there is anything weighing on our minds and making it difficult to focus, let us share it now and then let it go.

Enter a quiet time when family members can share. You might go first and set the example by sharing anything that is weighing on your own mind.

Listening for God

Say: The Scripture for today is found in a letter sent from Paul to his friend Timothy. In this letter, Paul reminds Timothy to pray for the people in leadership positions.

Read aloud 1 Timothy 2:1-7. Take turns reading the Scripture, or have a different family member read the Scripture passage each week.

 ## Family Share and Reflection Time

Say: Paul told Timothy to pray for people who are in leadership positions. We are going to create a prayer litany and pray together for the people who lead and guide our country, city, church, and family.

Activity: Make a list of people in leadership positions. Include people such as the president of our nation, senators, city officials, ministers, teachers, principals, and coaches, as well as the leaders of your own family. When you have completed your list, read each name aloud and respond as a family by saying, "God, give (name of individual) your wisdom to be a good leader."

Discussion Questions:
- Why do you think Paul told Timothy to pray for leaders?
- Why do you think it is important for us to pray for the leaders in our lives?
- When have you prayed for leaders in your life?
- Do you act as a leader for anyone? Does anyone follow you? Do you think their prayers might help you to be a better leader? Why or why not?

 **Asking God**

Say: Let us pray together as a family . . .

Let us share our prayers for the world—for our country and leaders, and for other countries and their leaders . . .

Let us share our prayers for the church, ministers, and other spiritual leaders . . .

Let us share our prayers for our friends, teachers, and others in our community . . .

Let us share our prayers for family members and our own specific needs . . .

Use the space provided below to make note of family prayer requests. Take a few minutes to review requests from the previous week.

Prayer Requests:

_____

_____

_____

_____

_____

Offering Ourselves to God

Pray aloud together:

God, we have read your Holy Word,
We have prayed together,
We have spent time with you,
We have experienced your love for us,

Now, we promise to love one another and others as you love us.
In the name of Christ. Amen.

Blessing One Another

Invite family members to bless one another. Some examples might be:

"May God bless you, guide you, and be with you, today and always. In the name of Christ, Amen."

"I love you, and I ask God to bless you."

"God loves you just the way you are, and so do I!"

GOD GIVES US WHAT WE NEED

"Strike the rock, and water will come out of it,
so that the people may drink."
—Exodus 17:6

Supplies

- Bible(s)
- sacred candle, matches or lighter
- bar of soap
- nail
- bowl
- pitcher of water
- *optional for older children, teens:* table knife

 ## Welcoming God

Gather as a family and light a candle as a symbolic way of inviting God to join you during this time together. Sit quietly for a moment so that everyone has the opportunity to relax his or her body, mind, and spirit.

Sharing With God

Say: If there is anything weighing on our minds and making it difficult to focus, let us share it now and then let it go.

Enter a quiet time when family members can share. You might go first and set the example by sharing anything that is weighing on your own mind.

Listening for God

Say: God used Moses to save the Hebrew people from slavery in Egypt, and they lived in the desert for forty years. At first they did not trust that God would take care of them in the desert. One time they were very thirsty and could not find water. They doubted that God would take care of them, and so Moses asked God to perform a miracle to show them that they had nothing to fear.

Read aloud Exodus 17:1-7. Take turns reading the Scripture, or have a different family member read the Scripture passage each week.

 Family Share and Reflection Time

Say: The people of God thought they were going to die of thirst. God told Moses to strike a rock, and water came out of it. Let's pretend this bar of soap is a rock. It is a symbol of our fears and doubts. One at a time, let's take turns digging into this soap until we break through and create a hole. As we dig, let's ask God to help us trust more fully.

Activity: Pass the bar of soap to each person, inviting him or her to dig into the soap with the nail. Once you have made a hole all the way through the soap, hold the soap over a bowl as you pour water through the hole. Remind your family that God will always take care of you whenever you need help. Place the soap near the bathroom or kitchen sink, inviting family members to recall every time they wash that God always takes care of you.

With older children and teens, have each one use a table knife to sculpt a bar of soap into a symbol of his or her fear. Have them place their sculptures in the shower and watch their fears disappear in the coming days!

Discussion Questions:

- Why do you think the Hebrew people doubted God in the desert? Do you think the rock taught them a lesson about God? What was it?
- Why do you think we sometimes doubt God? What can help us to trust God at all times?
- Has God ever answered a prayer or performed a miracle in your time of need?

 Asking God

Say: Let us pray together as a family . . .

Let us share our prayers for the world—for our country and leaders, and for other countries and their leaders . . .

Let us share our prayers for the church, ministers, and other spiritual leaders . . .

Let us share our prayers for our friends, teachers, and others in our community . . .

Let us share our prayers for family members and our own specific needs . . .

Use the space provided on the next page to make note of family prayer requests. Take a few minutes to review requests from the previous week.

Prayer Requests:

_____

_____

_____

_____

_____

Offering Ourselves to God

Pray aloud together:

> God, we have read your Holy Word,
> We have prayed together,
> We have spent time with you,
> We have experienced your love for us,
> Now, we promise to love one another and others as you
>   love us.
> In the name of Christ. Amen.

Blessing One Another

Invite family members to bless one another. Some examples might be:

> "May God bless you, guide you, and be with you, today
>   and always. In the name of Christ, Amen."

> "I love you, and I ask God to bless you."

> "God loves you just the way you are, and so do I!"

JESUS BLESSES THE CHILDREN

"Let the little children come to me; do not stop them;
for it is to such as these that the kingdom of God belongs."
—Mark 10:14

Supplies
- Bible(s)
- sacred candle, matches or lighter

 ## Welcoming God

Gather as a family and light a candle as a symbolic way of inviting God to join you during this time together. Sit quietly for a moment so that everyone has the opportunity to relax his or her body, mind, and spirit.

Sharing With God

Say: If there is anything weighing on our minds and making it difficult to focus, let us share it now and then let it go.

Enter a quiet time when family members can share. You might go first and set the example by sharing anything that is weighing on your own mind.

Listening for God

Say: In this story, parents brought their children to Jesus. The disciples did not understand how much Jesus loved children, and so they tried to send the children away. But Jesus loved the children. Let's see what happened!

Read aloud Mark 10:13-16. Take turns reading the Scripture, or have a different family member read the Scripture passage each week.

 Family Share and Reflection Time

Say: Jesus loved the children who were brought to him, and he loves children today just as much! Let's sing a song about how much Jesus loves each of us, God's children.

Activity: As a family, sing a modified version of "Jesus Loves Me" to each child in your family, substituting these words:

Jesus loves (name of child), this I know, for the Bible tells (us) so.
(Name of child) to him belongs.
(Name of child) is gentle and he is strong.
Yes, Jesus loves (name of child).
Yes, Jesus loves (name of child).
Yes, Jesus loves (name of child).
The Bible tells (us) so!

If you have teens in your family, skip the song and simply tell them how loved by Jesus they truly are! (Move on to the discussion questions, adapting them as necessary for the ages of your children.)

Discussion Questions:

- Why do you think the disciples tried to send the children away? Why do you think Jesus told them to let the children come to him?
- How did it feel to have this song sung to you? Was it comfortable or uncomfortable? Do you feel loved by Jesus? Why or why not?
- Do you think the phrase "child of God" refers only to those who are young in age, or do you think even old people are "children of God"? Why?

 Asking God

Say: Let us pray together as a family . . .

> Let us share our prayers for the world—for our country and leaders, and for other countries and their leaders . . .
>
> Let us share our prayers for the church, ministers, and other spiritual leaders . . .
>
> Let us share our prayers for our friends, teachers, and others in our community . . .
>
> Let us share our prayers for family members and our own specific needs . . .

Use the space provided on the next page to make note of family prayer requests. Take a few minutes to review requests from the previous week.

Prayer Requests:

_____

_____

_____

_____

_____

Offering Ourselves to God

Pray aloud together:

> God, we have read your Holy Word,
> We have prayed together,
> We have spent time with you,
> We have experienced your love for us,
> Now, we promise to love one another and others as you
>   love us.
> In the name of Christ. Amen.

Blessing One Another

Invite family members to bless one another. Some examples might be:

> "May God bless you, guide you, and be with you, today
>   and always. In the name of Christ, Amen."

> "I love you, and I ask God to bless you."

> "God loves you just the way you are, and so do I!"

ALL THINGS ARE POSSIBLE WITH GOD

"It is easier for a camel to go through the eye of a needle than for someone who is rich to enter the kingdom of God." —Mark 10:25

Supplies

- Bible(s)
- sacred candle, matches or lighter
- needle
- thread
- twine
- yarn
- pillow

Welcoming God

Gather as a family and light a candle as a symbolic way of inviting God to join you during this time together. Sit quietly for a moment so that everyone has the opportunity to relax his or her body, mind, and spirit.

Sharing With God

Say: If there is anything weighing on our minds and making it difficult to focus, let us share it now and then let it go.

Enter a quiet time when family members can share. You might go first and set the example by sharing anything that is weighing on your own mind.

Listening for God

Say: In this story, Jesus challenged a rich man to give up everything. This was a hard thing Jesus was asking him to do.
Then Jesus made a comment about a camel to remind his
listeners that all things are possible with God. While it is
hard to follow Jesus, it is possible! Let's hear the story.

Read aloud Mark 10:17-31. Take turns reading the Scripture, or
have a different family member read the Scripture passage each
week.

 Family Share and Reflection Time

Say: Jesus said it was easier for a camel to go through the eye
of a needle than for a rich man to follow God. This activity will help us see just how difficult following Jesus can
be.

Activity: Spend time inviting each family member to try to
thread a needle. Start with thread and move to larger things.
Enjoy this and let family members be silly! Keep reminding them
that Jesus spoke of trying to squeeze a camel through the eye of
a needle!

Discussion Questions:

- It was hard for the rich man to consider selling all he had
  to follow Jesus. Jesus said that all things are possible with
  God, so why do you think it was difficult for the rich man
  to follow Jesus?

- What things are difficult for you to do or give up for Jesus? Why?
- What would make it easier for you to do or give up these things?
- Is there anything our family can do to help you follow Jesus more closely?

 Asking God

Say: Let us pray together as a family . . .

Let us share our prayers for the world—for our country and leaders, and for other countries and their leaders . . .

Let us share our prayers for the church, ministers, and other spiritual leaders . . .

Let us share our prayers for our friends, teachers, and others in our community . . .

Let us share our prayers for family members and our own specific needs . . .

Use the space provided below to make note of family prayer requests. Take a few minutes to review requests from the previous week.

Prayer Requests:

_____

_____

_____

_____

_____

Offering Ourselves to God

Pray aloud together:

God, we have read your Holy Word,
We have prayed together,
We have spent time with you,
We have experienced your love for us,
Now, we promise to love one another and others as you
    love us.
In the name of Christ. Amen.

Blessing One Another

Invite family members to bless one another. Some examples
might be:

"May God bless you, guide you, and be with you, today
    and always. In the name of Christ, Amen."

"I love you, and I ask God to bless you."

"God loves you just the way you are, and so do I!"

GIVING TO GOD WHAT IS GOD'S

"Give therefore to the emperor the things that are the emperor's, and to God the things that are God's." —Matthew 22:21b

Supplies

- Bible(s)
- sacred candle, matches or lighter
- assortment of coins
- aluminum foil and toothpick for each family member

 ## Welcoming God

Gather as a family and light a candle as a symbolic way of inviting God to join you during this time together. Sit quietly for a moment so that everyone has the opportunity to relax his or her body, mind, and spirit.

Sharing With God

Say: If there is anything weighing on our minds and making it difficult to focus, let us share it now and then let it go.

Enter a quiet time when family members can share. You might go first and set the example by sharing anything that is weighing on your own mind.

Listening for God

Say: This story reminds us that Jesus told us to give to the world what belongs to the world and to God what belongs to God. He used a coin as a symbol.

Read aloud Matthew 22:15-22. Take turns reading the Scripture, or have a different family member read the Scripture passage each week.

 Family Share and Reflection Time

Say: People asked Jesus whom they should follow: the government or God. Jesus took a coin and used it to tell them that they could be part of the world and still love God. In this time together, we will design our own coins for God and write on them things we should give to God.

Activity: Spend time looking at real coins. Discuss why the people and symbols appearing on the coins were chosen. (Do some research in advance, if necessary.) Give each person a piece of aluminum foil and a toothpick for scratching or drawing symbols, and invite him or her to create a coin to honor God. The coin may be any shape. Spend time sharing the coins when everyone has finished.

Discussion Questions:
- Why did you choose the shape and symbols you did for your coin?
- Do you think we should give our time and energy to God and to other things, as well? Explain your answer.

- Do you think you give more time to God or to other things? Is the time you give to God enough? Why or why not?
- Are there changes you need to make in your life so that you will have more time for God?

 Asking God

Say: Let us pray together as a family . . .

> Let us share our prayers for the world—for our country and leaders, and for other countries and their leaders . . .
> Let us share our prayers for the church, ministers, and other spiritual leaders . . .
> Let us share our prayers for our friends, teachers, and others in our community . . .
> Let us share our prayers for family members and our own specific needs . . .

Use the space provided below to make note of family prayer requests. Take a few minutes to review requests from the previous week.

Prayer Requests:

_____

_____

_____

_____

_____

Offering Ourselves to God

Pray aloud together:

God, we have read your Holy Word,
We have prayed together,
We have spent time with you,
We have experienced your love for us,
Now, we promise to love one another and others as you
    love us.
In the name of Christ. Amen.

Blessing One Another

Invite family members to bless one another. Some examples
might be:

"May God bless you, guide you, and be with you, today
    and always. In the name of Christ, Amen."

"I love you, and I ask God to bless you."

"God loves you just the way you are, and so do I!"

WHAT HAVE WE SEEN?

Then Jesus said to him, "What do you want me to do for you?" The blind man said to him, "My teacher, let me see again." Jesus said to him, "Go; your faith has made you well." —Mark 10:51-52a

Supplies
- Bible(s)
- sacred candle, matches or lighter
- blindfold for every family member
- several bags—each with one odd object inside (Examples: peeled hardboiled egg, wet spaghetti noodles, shredded paper; be creative and choose things that family members will not immediately recognize by touching)

 ## Welcoming God

Gather as a family and light a candle as a symbolic way of inviting God to join you during this time together. Sit quietly for a moment so that everyone has the opportunity to relax his or her body, mind, and spirit.

Sharing With God

Say: If there is anything weighing on our minds and making it difficult to focus, let us share it now and then let it go.

Enter a quiet time when family members can share. You might go first and set the example by sharing anything that is weighing on your own mind.

Listening for God

Say: In this Scripture, Jesus heals a blind man. Let's hear the story.

Read aloud Mark 10:46-52. Take turns reading the Scripture, or have a different family member read the Scripture passage each week.

 # Family Share and Reflection Time

Say: In this story Jesus wanted to help a man to see even though others tried to send the man away. Jesus told him that his faith had made him well. Can you imagine how different things looked to this man once his vision was made clear? This activity is going to help us try to understand how important our eyesight really is.

Activity: Have everyone put on a blindfold. Then invite each family member to reach into the bags one at a time and try to figure out what is inside. Hopefully, they will have a difficult time guessing exactly what is in each bag. After everyone has had a few guesses, take off the blindfolds and see what is really in the bags.

Discussion Questions:
- Things seem very different when we cannot see them than when we actually see them. What object in the bags most surprised you?
- Now that we have been doing devotions together for all these weeks, do you "see" God and prayer and the Bible the same way that you used to, or are you seeing things in a new way? Explain.

- What new insights have you discovered through our times together?
- Do you plan to make any changes in your life, or have you already made changes, as a result of our being together each week?
- What should we do from this point forward? Should we stop meeting together? Should we continue gathering? How can we stay on our spiritual journey as a family?

 Asking God

Say: Let us pray together as a family . . .

Let us share our prayers for the world—for our country and leaders, and for other countries and their leaders . . .

Let us share our prayers for the church, ministers, and other spiritual leaders . . .

Let us share our prayers for our friends, teachers, and others in our community . . .

Let us share our prayers for family members and our own specific needs . . .

Use the space provided below to make note of family prayer requests. Take a few minutes to review requests from the previous week.

Prayer Requests:

_____

_____

_____

_____

_____

Offering Ourselves to God

Pray aloud together:

> God, we have read your Holy Word,
> We have prayed together,
> We have spent time with you,
> We have experienced your love for us,
> Now, we promise to love one another and others as you
> love us.
> In the name of Christ. Amen.

Blessing One Another

Invite family members to bless one another. Some examples
might be:

> "May God bless you, guide you, and be with you, today
> and always. In the name of Christ, Amen."

> "I love you, and I ask God to bless you."

> "God loves you just the way you are, and so do I!"